book is not only valuable, but needed. Make sure you read this informative and entertaining book."

— *Kim L. Collier, Author, Marketing Strategist and Founder of Brown Girls Who Write.*

"This book is a practical and powerful guide to achievement that will help the next generation of diverse rising stars get to the top faster in both their professional and personal lives."

— *Robert Hill, Pittsburgh-based Communications Consultant*

"Thomas Brooks masterfully devises a powerful motivational tool in *26.2 Ways to Do it Now*. After reading it, failure can NEVER be an option."

— *Marc Lacy, Speaker, Writer, Producer*

"Thomas Brooks is 'that guy' we admire from afar for what seems to be his golden, effortless touch. In this must-read masterpiece, he shares practical, relatable, and repeatable strategies for the next generation of entrepreneurs, executives, and advocates. Employ these timeless principles to successfully crush the "walls" we all encounter in this marathon called life."

— *Dr. mOe Anderson, Dentist, Author, Speaker, Advocate DrmOeanderson.com*

Praise for *26.2 Ways to Do It Now*

"This book is remarkable and exciting to read. This pragmatic guide will help many emerging leaders steer through these unpredictable times."

— Honorable Judge Kevin E. Cooper, Sr. (Retired)

"The life lessons in *26.2 Ways to Do It Now* provide emerging leaders with a compelling roadmap for business success and long-term happiness."

— Eric Lofholm, Bestselling Author and Master Sales Trainer

"A compelling vision for achieving sustainable personal and professional fulfillment, presented in a simultaneously entertaining and educational manner."

— Kornelia Tancheva, Ph.D.
Hillman University Librarian and Director, University of Pittsburgh Library System

"This book is a timely and needed addition to conversations about educational opportunity and student success. Thomas Brooks aptly utilizes his personal narrative to contextualize how ethnicity, education, privilege, and culture intersect and influence our present and our future. As a call to action, the author highlights how organizations can leverage Diversity and Inclusion, among other high impact practices, to spark creativity and high performance."

– Kenyatta N. Shamburger, Assistant Dean of Students for Intercultural Initiatives and Resource Centers, Iowa State University

"A thought-provoking perspective covering many aspects of personal development, success, and contentment."

– Judy Lubin, Ph.D., MPH, President, Center for Urban and Racial Equity (CURE)

"Thomas Brooks has granted all of us a real gift with *26.2 Ways to Do It Now*. The book will help many young professionals navigate these challenging times. I encourage everyone to incorporate his game-changing principles in their lives."

– Henry M. Goodgame Jr., Vice President, External Relations and Alumni Engagement at Morehouse College

"Thomas Brooks has written a must-read primer as a motivating professional development book to help others achieve their full potential. *26.2 Ways to Do It Now* is a delightful guide full of important information that can help rising stars reach the top."

– Toschia Moffett, Attorney, Author, Business Owner

"Thomas Brooks is the type of entrepreneur who has figured out how to combine business and fun. As an author and entrepreneur, this

26.2 WAYS TO DO IT NOW

Life Lessons for Happiness and Success

Thomas Brooks

Alpha Multimedia, Inc.
Houston, Texas, USA
www.AlphaMultimedia.com

ALPHA MULTIMEDIA
Marketing Matters

COPYRIGHT

Publisher's Cataloging-In-Publication Data

(Prepared by The Donohue Group, Inc.)

Names: Brooks, Thomas, 1966- author.

Title: 26.2 ways to do it now : life lessons for happiness and success / Thomas Brooks.

Other Titles: Twenty-six point two ways to do it now

Description: Houston, Texas, USA : Alpha Multimedia, Inc., [2021] | Series: Family success series ; [2] | Interest age level: 14 and up. | Summary: This book provides encouragement and guidance to anyone seeking improvement and achievement in their lives. In addition to true stories from his own life, Brooks provides quotes and examples of the principles in action in the lives of famous individuals. Applying these principles will help one to achieve happiness and success.

Identifiers: ISBN 9780977462902 (paperback) | ISBN 9780977462919 (Kindle) | ISBN 9780977462926 (ePDF)

Subjects: LCSH: Success--Anecdotes--Juvenile literature. | Success in business--Anecdotes--Juvenile literature. | Happiness--Anecdotes--Juvenile literature. | Achievement motivation in adolescence--Anecdotes--Juvenile literature. | Self-actualization (Psychology)--Anecdotes--Juvenile literature. | Brooks, Thomas, 1966---Anecdotes--Juvenile literature. | CYAC: Success--Anecdotes. | Success in business--Anecdotes. | Happiness--Anecdotes. | Achievement motivation--Anecdotes. | Self-actualization (Psychology)--Anecdotes. | Brooks, Thomas, 1966---Anecdotes. | LCGFT: Self-help publications.

Classification: LCC BF624.3.S9 B76 2021 (print) | LCC BF624.3.S9 (ebook) | DDC 158.10835--dc23

DEDICATION

This book is dedicated to my adoptive mother, Joan Brooks. Because of Joan's love and the many sacrifices she made, she is my mother in the truest sense of the word, just as if she delivered me from her own womb. While raising me, she always put my needs above her own. Joan Brooks dedicated herself to giving me a strong foundation in life. Though she is no longer with us, I will love her always.

ACKNOWLEDGEMENT

I want to show gratitude to some of the people who have encouraged me to finish this project.

My wife, Nikki, provided an abundance of love and encouragement to help me finish the manuscript. I am incredibly grateful to her for the unflinching support and for the family we created.

My son, Joshua – who was about to leave home to start his Freshman year of college – provided helpful insights from a Gen Z perspective. I love him, I am proud of him, and I am his biggest fan.

My daughter, Kendall, is delightful. I love her, and she inspires me, each day, to be a better man.

My amazing birth mother, Dorothy Wallstein, I am proud of who she is and what she has done. I love her. She is a positive force in my life.

My loving, caring sisters, Lotus Hannon and Margaret Omwenga, I say thank you to you both for all your help on this project and in general.

My marvelous cousins, Tammy Lowry Gault, Christy Lewis, and Kyra Smith, you are among the very best cousins in the world.

My distinguished Brothers of Alpha Phi Alpha Fraternity, Inc., including Dr. Vaughn Clagette, Brett Fontenot, Jon Gee, Steven Gourrier, Elridge Guillory, Dr. Andre Hall, James Harrison, Dr.

Alfred B. Henson, Todd Hood, and Arty Sheffield, you're the best crew – ice cold Brothers – and I'm grateful to have you all!

My dynamic business partners, Lillie Fontenot, Monica Fontenot-Poindexter, April Lloyd, and Robin Tillmon, you're a support team I cherish very dearly.

My incredible, supportive, and crazy-cool friends, Gerard Andrews, Reggie Bush, Tia Collins, Cynthia Daly, Valerie Durant, Cynthia Ginyard, Toni Jackman, Lynnae Jackson, Trina Love, Crystal McCormick, Jill McGavin, Brad Michael, Ginger Miller, Monica Miller, Sean Ryan, Sherri Sims, Natasha Stevens, and Taylor Thierry, I wake up thankful every morning for the gift of you all in my life.

TABLE OF CONTENTS

INTRODUCTION

I had the idea, at least four years ago, to write this, my second book. I planned a written digest of life lessons that enable both happiness in life and success in business. However, the words flowed slowly while I focused on other business endeavors, my growing children, deaths in our extended family, recovering from a detached retina, and global travel, instead of accelerating the creation of this book.

And then, early in 2020, the whole world began to be impacted by the tragic COVID-19 pandemic. Millions of confirmed cases were reported, and a horrific number of people died. In the business world, large, established companies had enormous layoffs. Many small businesses either folded or struggled to remain open. Schools closed, which resulted in my son finishing his senior year of high school from home. His senior year of track and field competition was wiped out after only two meets. My daughter finished middle school through online instruction while desperately missing her friends and teachers.

Former U.S. president, John Adams, once said, *"Every problem is an opportunity in disguise."* Since my regular social life and international travel got put on hold, I had extra time in my schedule to dedicate to writing and completing this manuscript. I am so glad I wrote this book in 2020 instead of four years earlier. Over the last four years, my experiences have yielded a much better book than what I would have created previously. The life lessons provided in this book are especially timely, given the challenging times we face, both in America and globally.

My inspiration and strategy were simple. Former U.S. president, Abraham Lincoln, once declared, *"Leave nothing for tomorrow, which can be done today."* In addition, motivational speaker and author, Brian Tracy, stated, *"Move fast. A sense of urgency is the one thing you can develop that will separate you from everyone else. When you get a good idea, **do it now.**"* So, I adopted the motto, "Do It Now!" I just blocked off time on my calendar and wrote for two hours each day. I got the book written, and I used the same motto as part of my book title.

When I was younger, I ran and finished five marathons – the full 26.2 miles or, more specifically, 26 miles plus 385 yards. Never forget the final 385 yards. I learned a lot about life by training for and completing these grueling long-distance events.

Life is a marathon, not a sprint.

Why is a marathon a good *metaphor* for life? In a marathon, only one person gets 1st place in a particular category or age group; for example, Female 18-29. However, there are many people who *effectively win* their own individual race. For example, some people are happy to complete the entire event – regardless of their finishing time – because they get the benefits of stronger muscles and cardiovascular fitness. For yet another reason, some other people are happy because they improved and achieved a new personal best time. Life is similar to a marathon. Your victory may be different from my victory, yet we can all grow and win.

In the world of running, they joke that when you get to Mile 20, you are halfway done with the marathon. That math does not work, so why do they say that? It is because the *effort needed* to tackle Miles 1 to 20 is roughly equal to the effort required to finish Miles 21 to 26.2.

Naturally, when your body needs energy, it can draw on its glycogen stores. These molecules, made from glucose in the food you eat, are mainly stored in your liver and muscles. However, for marathoners, there is a concept called "hitting the wall". In long-distance running, this is a condition of sudden exhaustion, which occurs when you consume nearly all of the glycogen stores in your muscles. Basically, you look and feel good one minute, and then you abruptly run out of gas – typically around Mile 20.

I enjoy long-distance running because it builds endurance, confidence, and mental toughness. Another benefit of vigorous exercise is that your body typically reacts by releasing chemicals called endorphins. Scientists tell us that endorphins trigger a positive feeling in the body, similar to that of some narcotics. After a strenuous workout or run, one often feels elated. That sensation, commonly known as a "runner's high," can be accompanied by a positive and energizing outlook on life.

However, despite my training, I "hit the wall" in three of my five marathons. On one of these suboptimal occasions, I ran during an ice storm and ended up with hypothermia. I struggled mightily during the last 6.2 miles. My body temperature eventually dropped under 95°F, and I ended up in the Medical Area after crossing the finish line. I could not stop shivering for more than an hour after the race, even after changing into dry clothes. Though I trained hard for five months before that marathon, I, unfortunately, caught the flu about three weeks before the race. The flu lingered, and my recovery was slow. However, I did not want to "waste" five months of training by not doing my scheduled race. I thought I had fully recuperated, only to discover that I was not at 100% strength on race day. That, when combined with the damp and cold ice storm conditions, left me in a troubling situation.

Similarly, in life, a lot of people who look good in terms of grades, college acceptances, and internships at age 18 or 19 eventually hit a "wall" – like a marathoner who begins to struggle at Mile 20 – and then they are not in good condition once they reach their late twenties and beyond. To extend the metaphor, in both life and running, your daily course is rarely perfect or ideal. However, you can challenge yourself every day when you step up to the starting line. Through hard work and learning new skills, you can grow and reach your goal.

On that note, in my very next marathon after the ice storm incident, I cruised right past the so-called "wall" and finished in 3 hours, 11 minutes and 28 seconds – an average pace of 7 minutes, 19 seconds per mile, my personal best for the full marathon. How did I do it? I had trained consistently, leveraged massage therapy to avoid injury, carefully managed my diet, and avoided catching a cold or flu. In short, it was my "Six P's" in action that I generally apply to my life – not only marathon running – *proper prior planning promotes peak performance!*

Not everyone runs a marathon, but everyone does live a life. This book is about life lessons for happiness and success. Like a marathon runner, the way you rebound after a setback makes all the difference. Like a marathoner, you can only reach your goals through persistence and discipline. Like a marathoner, you must learn from your mistakes and – if you are smart – the mistakes of others. Like a marathoner, you will need a burning desire directed toward your goals and dreams.

This book provides concrete advice, delivered through *26.2 modular chapters, that can each stand on their own* as part of the roadmap to hard-earned triumphs that delight your soul. So, feel free to read the book straight through, or you can skip around to various chapters if you want.

And if you are not really into the marathon running thing, then think of the 26 chapters as a metaphor for the roughly 26 annual paychecks you get every two weeks from your job. If you master these 26.2 life lessons over the next 12 months, the rewards will be greater than your paycheck.

I endeavor to encourage and guide anyone seeking personal and professional improvement. Folks ranging from 14 to 34 years of age are most likely to embrace these life lessons; however, most of the standalone chapters can be helpful to those of almost any age.

In addition to using compelling stories from my own life and career, I have also included quotes and examples of the principles in action in the lives of famous individuals, many of whom you will recognize.

You probably already know that if you do what you have always done, you will continue to get the result you have always gotten. Apply these 26.2 lessons to your own life and access the treasures of sustainable happiness and success that await you at the finish line.

Thomas Brooks
August 2020

CHAPTER ONE

START WITH THE VISION

*"The only thing worse than being
blind is having sight and no vision."*

— Helen Keller, author and political activist

Vision is seeing the future as you want it to be. Visionaries have a
knack for seeing possibilities that are hidden from others and believe
it is inevitable that the vision will be realized. This belief puts them in
action. You need enough imagination to recognize advantageous
opportunities. Having a vision provides the intended purpose and
direction for an organization or an individual. Your vision will help
you develop your objectives and guide the choices you make during
your journey. Therefore, companies must have a grand vision. Non-
profit organizations must have a strong vision. And, for your own
personal development, *you* need to have a vision – what you see for
your own world that you are creating.

In one of my much-loved parables described in *The Story Factor* by
Annette Simmons, a traveler in medieval times comes upon a
stonemason at work. He asks, "What are you doing?" The man looks

weary and unhappy. He responds, "Can't you see I am cutting and laying down stone? My back is killing me, and I can't wait to stop."

The traveler continues on his way and comes upon a second stonemason. "What are you doing?" he asks. "I'm building a wall," says the stonemason. "I'm grateful to have this work so I can support my family," he enthused.

As the traveler walks on, he encounters a third stonemason who seems to be doing exactly the same work as the previous two. He asks the third man, "What are you doing?" The man stands up straight, with a radiant face. He looks up at the sky and spreads his arms wide. "I am building a cathedral," he answers. His struggle had meaning.

As a practical matter, the three workers are basically doing the same work – laying the stones for a structure. However, the story they tell themselves and the traveler about their labor shapes how they feel, and most likely, the quality of their work. The first man had a job, the second man had a career, while the third man had a *vision*.

A strong vision can produce and sustain passion. A powerful vision can give you the energy to continue when obstacles present themselves. And if you passionately believe in your vision, you can rally others around it and get them to commit to it.

> **Life Lesson:**
> A powerful vision can give you the energy
> to continue when obstacles present themselves.
> And if you passionately believe in your vision,
> you can rally others.

A classic example is a speech by U.S president, John F. Kennedy, in 1961, where he said, *"I believe that this nation should commit itself to achieving the goal, before this decade is out, of landing a man on the moon and returning him safely to the earth."*

And in a subsequent speech, Kennedy said, *"But why, some say, the moon? Why choose this as our goal? And they may well ask why climb the highest mountain? Why, 35 years ago, fly the Atlantic? Why does Rice play Texas? We choose to go to the moon in this decade and do the other things, not because they are easy, but because they are hard, because that goal will serve to organize and measure the best of our energies and skills, because that challenge is one that we are willing to accept, one we are unwilling to postpone, and one which we intend to win, and the others, too."*

Kennedy's statements had everything anyone needs when crafting a vision for themselves or for their organization – Kennedy's vision answered the questions of who, what, when, where, and why. All that was left for the scientists at NASA was to figure out the *how* of getting the moonshot done.

A subsequent story tells of Kennedy visiting the NASA Space Center in Houston. President Kennedy, apparently, took a wrong turn and ended up in a hallway.

There, Kennedy noticed a janitor carrying a broom. Kennedy said, "Hi, I'm Jack Kennedy. What are you doing?" The janitor replied: "Well, Mr. President, I'm helping to put a man on the moon."

This worker had embraced the vision. He was not just a janitor cleaning a building; he was assisting as history was being made. Imagine how the janitor must have felt in July 1969 when Apollo 11 astronaut, Neil Armstrong, made 'one giant leap for mankind', and then subsequently returned safely to earth.

It does not matter how significant or tiny your current role may be; you are adding to the larger narrative evolving within your company, your team, your community, your family, and your life. Yes, the janitor got it. He fully understood the vision, his part in it, and he had a purpose.

I was only two years old when the Apollo 11 mission landed astronauts on the moon. However, during my career in high tech, I have come in contact with a number of people and engineering companies that had something to do with the Apollo 11 mission. Motorola did much of the communications equipment; IBM delivered the computational power required for the mission to be successful, while General Motors provided guidance systems and batteries that powered the lunar module. Westinghouse Electric Corporation, my former employer, developed the camera that captured the images of the surface of the moon. Texas Instruments, another of my former employers, provided switches that were on the ground in the control center and hundreds more that were aboard the spacecraft.

Inspired by Kennedy's vision, all these companies and their tens of thousands of individual engineers, technicians, and craftspeople pushed the boundaries of technology.

My father-in-law, Lenel Walton, was one of those heroes. He worked as a technician in Huntsville, Alabama, for McDonnell Douglas on a project for the Saturn V rocket. It was the Saturn V that launched Apollo 11, putting a man on the moon.

A vision is a direction, not a current-state reality. This means we work in pursuit of achieving our vision. Great leaders generate a vision, communicate the vision, and persistently drive it until the vision is accomplished. They do this for their organization and for themselves.

Life Lesson:

A vision is a direction, not a current-state reality. This means we work in pursuit of achieving our vision. Great leaders generate and communicate a vision.

These days, many companies, sometimes, feel that it is too much effort to galvanize employees around a company's vision. And a lot of companies think it is even tougher to get Millennials (a.k.a. Gen Y, born 1981 to 1996) to rally around the organization's vision. Millennials are often stereotyped as habitual job-hoppers. In reality, Millennials are often steadfastly devoted to people and causes rather than to the company itself. A case in point is that I have spoken to scores of Millennials, and none of the ones I talked with are looking to work for just one company for their whole career and then retire.

Most Millennials are used to enduring company reorganizations almost every year. They expect to change careers multiple times. So, there is rarely loyalty to the company. Millennials tend to be guided by their personal reason and values. They are typically more passionate about the world they want to create.

So, what is the implication for organizations? Millennials typically have a personal vision for their lives, and they hope to work for companies and teams that have visions that align with their own. Instead of writing off the retention of talented Millennials as a lost cause, businesses must 'pitch' themselves to potential employees. Businesses/companies must 'sell' their visions to Millennials to retain and inspire top talent across their organizations.

When developing an individual vision statement – whether you are in Gen X, a Xennial, a Millennial, or a Gen Z – it is imperative to outline your aspirations and talents. What are your skills, and how might those skills be useful in your next role? Do these skills you enjoy possess such a value that the world is willing to pay handsomely for them? What kind of world would you like to live in? How can you serve that vision?

And while you develop your vision statement, consider the values you cherish. What is your vision for your health? What is your vision for your wealth? Do you value life balance and family fun? Do you want to be a leader? How do you want to give service to others, and how will that service create the world you wish to live in? What causes are you most passionate about?

> **Life Lesson:**
>
> As you develop your vision statement, consider your values. How do you want to give service to others? How will that service create the world you wish to live in?

The result of answering these challenging questions is a vision statement that supports both your life goals and your career goals.

Just as NASA faced challenges and difficulties during the space race of the 1960s, you will also face adversity, but a strong vision can help you weather the inevitable storms that will arise. In those moments of adversity, focus on moving toward your vision. Channel your energy into the wonderful future you are creating.

My personal vision is: "Good health, life balance, fun, fulfilling relationships, autonomy, community service, legacy, financial security, and longevity."

I am thrilled to wake up each day to make progress toward the realization of my vision. I hope you are, too. Let's do it now!

"Go confidently in the direction of your dreams! Live the life you've imagined. As you simplify your life, the laws of the universe will be simpler."

— Henry David Thoreau, essayist,
poet, and philosopher

#DoItNow – What Actions Will You Take as a Result of Reading This Chapter?
1)
2)
3)

CHAPTER TWO

DEFINITE MAJOR PURPOSE

"There is one quality, which one must possess to win, and that is definiteness of purpose, the knowledge of what one wants, and a burning desire to possess it."

— Napoleon Hill, author and lecturer

The recipe for success is simple but not easy.

Vision – as detailed in Chapter One – is about seeing the future as you want it to be. Your vision helps you develop your objectives and guide the choices you make during your journey. Vision enables you to try on your Definite Major Purpose (DMP) in your mind before you finalize it. Vision lets you experience the emotions of accomplishing *your primary goal* and any other goals before you even begin the journey. Vision is what you see for your world, and your DMP is a big part of that.

As Napoleon Hill described in *Think and Grow Rich*, the formula for achievement is clear:

$$DMP + PMA + WPOA + MMA = Success$$

DMP refers to the one thing for which you have a burning desire. Your Definite Major Purpose is not something that you simply want; it is something you deeply crave. Make your DMP the one strategic objective that is most important to you right now. And it is usually the one primary objective that enables you to determine your priorities for any other goals and activities.

Life Lesson:

Your Definite Major Purpose (DMP) should be something you deeply crave. Make your DMP the one strategic objective that is most important to you right now.

If you were guaranteed success in any area where you can put a singular focus, what would it be? What would you do if you had a bottomless cup of time and resources? What is your top passion in life? What is the one thing that will get you up and out of bed each morning? If you can earn money while following your passion, you will generally feel like you are not working at all. You would be leading a life that you love. What are the most important things you want to accomplish in your lifetime? After you have your DMP in place, there will be some benefits. For example, you can organize your personal development efforts around your initiative, creativity, zeal, and self-discipline to achieve that DMP.

Some people have a DMP around financial freedom. Others want to leave the world of corporate America so they can teach or join the Peace Corps. What is it that you deeply desire?

Let me use myself as an example of putting this formula into action.

> *In the first half of 2020, my Definite Major Purpose was to help, by the end of 2023, tens of thousands of people, directly and indirectly, using my growing business as a catapult for their own success. Tactically, I wanted to complete the manuscript for this – my second book – and subsequently use the finished book to get more paid speaking engagements and bookings to deliver online training events. Now, more than ever, with the completion of this publication, I get booked to speak on topics, including Leadership, Diversity and Inclusion, and Networking for Success, with my two books acting as calling cards. In addition, this work on my book will inspire and enable me to create enough weekly blog posts on AlphaMultimedia.com to last at least two years, which means more free content on my blog, allowing me to help thousands of more people.*

PMA stands for Positive Mental Attitude. When we have a personal philosophy of positivity, we are much more likely to find ways to be successful and accomplish our dreams. It also helps that a Positive Mental Attitude is contagious and can influence other people on your team, in your community, and in your family.

Life Lesson:

When we have a personal philosophy of positivity, we are much more likely to find ways to be successful and accomplish our dreams.

A negative attitude is also contagious, but it pulls people in the wrong direction. By the way, for every cloud, there is a silver lining. All your troubles and obstacles are blessings in disguise when you approach your challenges with a positive mental attitude. It is also worth noting that in your conscious mind, you can only think about one thing at a time. If a negative thought enters your conscious mind, just proactively think of an affirmation or a positive mantra, or you can focus on any fond memory from your past.

> *I am generally a positive guy. For me, in 2020, I felt very confident that this book would help people navigate these challenging times. I got my wife enrolled in this vision and my Definite Major Purpose. And my Positive Mental Attitude helped me engage with friends and allies who would encourage me. For example, at one point, I had three different options on the design of the front cover of this book. Using social media, I got nearly 100 people to provide feedback on the various options. The feedback was extremely helpful, and it started with me projecting a positive vision for my project. Even at the beginning, I knew I would end up with a great cover design.*

> *I did the same thing when I was seeking out reviews and endorsements. My Positive Mental Attitude makes it easier for people to want to help me.*

WPOA stands for Written Plan of Action. Write down your objectives, strategies, and tactics if you want to reach your dreams. Put those tactics in your calendar, whether you use an electronic or hardcopy calendar. If you do not schedule the task, it is not real. And worse yet, it is unlikely to ever get done.

> *Once I got rolling on this project, having a Written Plan of Action allowed me to get it done quickly. To complete the manuscript, I not only committed to writing at least two hours per day, I also*

blocked that time in my calendar. I also put in my calendar all the other related tasks, including creating a Kindle™ version of this book, updates to my website, and public relations tactics.

Life Lesson:

Write down your objectives, strategies, and tactics if you want to reach your dreams. Put those tactics in your calendar. If you do not schedule the task, it is not real.

MMA refers to a Master Mind Alliance. This is the team that believes the same as you and supports you in reaching your goal. The people that comprise your Master Mind Alliance might be your employees, colleagues, business partners, family, and/or mentors.

To complete this book, my Master Mind Alliance was essential. My wife, Nikki, was there with love and support, and she read all my draft chapters. My Gen Z son provided his opinions, as well, and he made this book much better through his thoughtful questions. My birth mother and two of my sisters made amazing contributions. I bounced ideas off of numerous cousins, fraternity brothers, business partners, and friends.

The result was that I was able to utilize their experience, viewpoint, education, and expertise as if they were my own, leading to a much better book in the end.

Life Lesson:

Everyone needs a Master Mind Alliance. This is the team that believes the same as you and that supports you in reaching your goal.

You must *decide* what you really want and that you will reach that goal. Just as homicide means to kill a person, the word decide effectively means to kill off the other options. You are telling yourself that you will not fail to achieve your DMP, no matter what may come. Figuratively speaking, you and your army have invaded foreign territory and "burned the boats," demonstrating that you are serious and committed. There is no turning back. This gives you and your team no other option besides success. And when setting your DMP, you want to aim high. Shoot for the stars; if you do not make it, maybe you at least hit the moon.

Having a DMP means you must give up some things. The old saying is, "There's no free lunch." For example, let's say you're an entrepreneur building a business part-time. You may have to give up much of your "screen time" to be successful. By screen time, I am referring not only to time spent watching TV, but also time wasted aimlessly on social media and streaming content such as Netflix to any of your devices. This "screen time" can be a distraction that keeps us from thinking and using our creativity. It can also take unnecessary time away from our loved ones. Be present. This is the only life you get; it is not a dress rehearsal. And giving up just five hours per week of screen time can make a big difference for a part-time business owner.

The fundamental Law of Karma is that every action and every choice have a consequence. We are always making decisions. Even indecision is actually a decision.

A story told by novelist, Marc Levy, touches on the consequences of not living in the present and the need to make the most of each day. Imagine you woke up every morning with a brand new $86,400 in your bank account, but you cannot carry the money over to the next day. You must use it, or the bank deletes it. You would spend it all, right?

Or, as Denzel Washington once tweeted, *"If you had $86,400 and someone stole $60, would you throw away $86,340 for revenge? Or move on and live? Each of us have 86,400 seconds every day. Don't let someone's negative 60 seconds ruin the remaining 86,340."*

We have a choice on what we do with those 86,400 seconds every day. The concept most people call "time management" has little basis in reality. Winners manage themselves by controlling their thoughts. Others try to manage time, which typically has little impact. Yes, we can make plans and fine-tune our schedule, but the hands on the clock just keep moving. We get 86,400 seconds every day. Even Oprah, Bill Gates, and any other powerful or famous person you can think of only get 86,400 seconds every day. The bigger payback is from *priority management*, so live life on purpose. And there is no bigger priority than your own DMP.

Passion and your DMP are related. Martin Luther King, Jr. was passionate about the belief that all people should have equal rights and not be judged by their skin color but by their character.

Thurgood Marshall was passionate in his desire to apply the principles of the U.S. Constitution to all Americans, not just to white people. By the time Marshall was nominated to become a Supreme Court justice in 1967, few lawyers in history had argued — and won — more cases before the nation's highest court. He racked up 29 wins (against just three losses), including his most famous victory, *Brown v. Board of Education*, the 1954 momentous decision that forced public schools to desegregate. He was the first African American appointed as a Supreme Court Justice, and he served for 24 years, until 1991. Marshall is the most pivotal lawyer in the destruction of Jim Crow, and therefore the most important lawyer of the 20th century.

Winston Churchill was passionate that England would push back and defeat Nazi Germany. We can also look at Franklin D. Roosevelt, Abraham Lincoln, and Nelson Mandela as other examples of passionate leaders who had a specific DMP.

Hill taught us in *Think and Grow Rich* that there are nine basic motives: love, sex, material/financial gain, self-preservation, freedom, self-expression, life after death, anger/revenge, and fear. Note that seven of the nine are positive, and two are negative motives. Think about the great leaders that you admire. Think about which of these motivates the leaders I mentioned? Which of these nine are motives for you?

Shakespeare wrote, *"Our doubts are traitors, and make us lose the good we oft might win, by fearing to attempt."* With a Positive Mental Attitude, we let go of the doubts. With a strong Definite Major Purpose, we overcome the fear and procrastination that stops us from acting now, based on our Written Plan of Action. Remember, taking intentional, purposeful action consistent with your DMP extinguishes procrastination, and our Master Mind Alliance gives us encouragement or a kick in the rear when we get stuck.

When we stick to the formula, the results are success, happiness, and fulfillment. Just do it now!

> "Very few people or companies can clearly articulate WHY they do WHAT they do. By WHY I mean your purpose, cause, or belief - WHY does your company exist? WHY do you get out of bed every morning? And WHY should anyone care?"

— Simon Sinek, author of the book, *Start with Why*

#DoItNow – What Actions Will You Take as a Result of Reading This Chapter?
1)
2)
3)

CHAPTER THREE

EDUCATION IS THE PASSPORT TO THE FUTURE

"Education is the passport to the future, for tomorrow belongs to those who prepare for it today."

— Malcolm X, civil rights leader and human rights activist

Though I grew up in relative poverty with a struggling single mom, I put in the hard work to excel academically at my public high school in New Brighton, Pennsylvania. Figuratively speaking, I was *hungry*, and I did not want to stay stuck in the narrative of not having as much, wanting more, and experiencing a lack of access because of resources. At the age of six, I knew I wanted to go to college. I saw education as the passport to improve my financial future. Since my loving mother did not have the money to send me to college, I eventually figured out that the best way for me to get financing for college was to get all A's in middle school and then in high school. I was not perfect, but on most of my report cards, I earned a 4.0 GPA to reach my goal.

In high school, I studied on the bus on the way to road basketball games and track meets while my teammates were playing around. I often did my homework over lunch. Dating was not a priority while I was in high school. Being highly ranked academically in your high school class, at that time in western Pennsylvania, was not typically associated with being cool or having charm with the ladies at the high school level. Some of my friends called me "Knowledge Nut," "Brainiac," and other funny names.

I graduated as the valedictorian of my class and had several college options. I attended my first-choice school, the University of Pittsburgh – affectionately known as Pitt. As a result of my efforts in high school, I earned numerous scholarships that allowed me to complete my Pitt Bachelor of Science in Electrical Engineering degree free of charge. My figurative passport was now stamped with my entry visa – welcome to a brighter future!

For decades, people have complained that the SAT test is culturally biased. However, there are some socioeconomic biases in the educational process, as well. Although I completed my undergraduate degree at the University of Pittsburgh tuition free, there was an intangible cost, which was emotional. I had no frame of reference as to what to expect at college. No friend or family member had ever come back from college over Christmas break or for the summer to tell this disadvantaged kid details or give advice about their college experiences.

A case in point occurred during my first few days at Pitt. I went to my classes and received the required syllabuses. Each syllabus, of course, noted the required textbooks for the course. Every day, I just sat there, waiting for the professors to hand out the books so I could start doing the reading assignments that were the subject of their lectures. During the first few days of classes, I saw this big line outside the university book center. The window displays of the Book Center displayed best-selling fictional novels and Pitt paraphernalia, not the course textbooks, which filled the inside of the store. Thus, I had no idea that I was supposed to get in line with the other students and purchase textbooks. I assumed the lines were full of new students waiting to buy Pitt paraphernalia before Saturday's big football season opener. It never occurred to me that the lines were full of students buying textbooks for their classes.

Three days after I first noticed the lines, I asked a student coming from the bookstore why the lines were so long. I listened in disbelief. Do I really have to *buy* my own books? Deeply embarrassed, I returned to my room for my syllabuses, took my place in line, entered the sweating crowd, and ultimately bought my textbooks. Luckily, I had just received my last check from that summer's internship, so I was able to afford the unplanned purchase of the textbooks.

I stayed focused on advancing my education and career. After I entered corporate America and was an engineer for a while, I wanted to earn a Master of Business Administration (MBA) degree. I ended up going to business school part-time while still working full-time as an engineer. Fortunately, my employer paid for my tuition, so I earned my MBA without incurring any student loans. After a long day of work, I would commute about one hour from my job near Baltimore's BWI Airport down I-95 to the University of Maryland in College Park. I grabbed fast food in College Park, ate in my car, and then went to class from 7 p.m. to 10 p.m. I did this for two to three nights per week for over two and a half years. I spent my free evenings studying or meeting with fellow students on my business case teams. There was no time for fun in those years. Once again, I was *hungry* to learn, grow, and achieve.

So, essentially, all my education was free – though I would say that I actually earned it. These academic degrees enabled me to have a successful career and a relatively comfortable lifestyle for my family. These days, while some question the value of a college degree, education made an *incredible difference* for me, and my education still pays huge dividends to this day. Ben Franklin said, "If a man empties his purse into his head, no man can take it away from him. An investment in knowledge always pays the best interest."

I advise you to be a life-long learner regardless of the degrees you pursue and complete. It only makes sense because, over time, technologies, best practices, and cultures evolve.

> **Life Lesson:**
> I advise you to be a life-long learner regardless
> of the degrees you pursue and complete.

If you specifically want to "answer the call" and pursue higher education, completing an undergraduate degree, and, hopefully, a master's degree, there are some things that you will want to take with you on your journey.

The Ability to Handle Academic Rigor

Students need to have the talent, academic skills, and self-discipline to handle demanding undergraduate and graduate coursework. Note that Chapter Five covers self-discipline in detail.

Direction and Purpose

Know where you are going. Students must set career goals and make choices that support their Definite Major Purpose, the *main thing* that you desire out of life. Your education should reflect your purpose, which ties into your career or entrepreneurial objectives. In Chapter Two, we covered the concept of your Definite Major Purpose (DMP).

The major reason my son, Joshua, worked hard in high school was that his own career goals inspired him. However, many students have no vision for their future careers; thus, the academic studies seem less relevant. This can be combatted by having more Career Days, where local professionals come and speak to the students. Or, better yet, more days when students can visit local workplaces that match their career interests. To accelerate your educational pursuits, find a way to create an inspiring vision of your future career or entrepreneurial life.

As a society, I hope we can find more pathways for corporate America to partner with high schools and invest in our children's futures through training, internships, externships, and apprenticeships. We would then have a chance to rewrite the future of American education, which is especially helpful in traditionally underserved communities. When I worked at Texas Instruments, the company had an excellent program where they built a relationship with a local high school in the Houston area. This afforded several seniors with strong academic backgrounds the opportunity to do a part-time internship. Those students gained great experience, which they could use to get future full-time internships. The experience was also helpful in scholarship applications. Additionally, the wise students that took advantage of this program had a better idea of what they really wanted to study in college.

Belief and Confidence

Students should have faith in themselves that they can overcome any obstacles to reach their potential and achieve their dreams – chapter Twenty-Two details how you can have extraordinary confidence.

Life Lesson:

Students should have faith in themselves that they can overcome any obstacles to reach their potential and achieve their dreams.

Finances

Formal education costs money. The financial aid process for college can seem quite scary. However, unless your mom, dad, or extended family can write a big check, you will probably have to tackle the process. You want to get as much "free money" – scholarships and grants – as possible while ruthlessly minimizing student loan debt. If you want scholarships, the best time to start demonstrating stellar academic performance is in middle school and then continuing to excel through high school. The second-best time to start crushing it academically is *right now*. If you are in college now and facing student loans, perform at an elite level over the next one or two semesters. New opportunities for scholarships will often open up.

The process kicks off with the Free Application for Federal Student Aid, also known as the FAFSA. Every year, the federal government offers well over $100 billion in grants, loans, and work-study funds to assist our future college graduates. But because the FAFSA is exceedingly long and confusing, about half of the students who would be eligible for aid do not even submit an application. Do not be that student that does not complete the FAFSA.

I will not attempt to write a comprehensive guide to financial aid here. However, I will say that if you are proactive and passionate about your educational dreams, you can find a way. Besides the federal government funding that some students do not try for, there are also thousands upon thousands of scholarships out there – with applications accessible simply by savvy searches on Google. If you are tall or short, there are scholarships for you. If you or your ancestors are part of a certain ethnic group, there is money for you. If you belong to a religious community or if you are agnostic, you can find funds. The searching and applications do take *significant time*, but if you start no later than your junior year of high school, you can improve your chances.

Start early. You should apply for hundreds of scholarships and grants. Putting the "Six P's" in action (Proper Prior Planning Promotes Peak Performance) can help you deal with the challenges some families must face. Over the long term, as a society, we can lobby for the universities to provide more help by flattening tuition increases and freeing up more money for scholarships and grants. As an example of the implications for families, some aspiring college students have a sibling with special needs. And such a diagnosis can have financial implications for the family. The parents may have to spend a lot on medical care and other support, such as speech or physical therapy. To help families with special circumstances, and even those without special circumstances who just do not have the money, we need more scholarships and grants made available through philanthropy and public universities. For example, some public schools, such as Texas A&M, currently have an endowment of over $13 billion. And the endowment at Harvard, a private school, is over $40 billion. Though some of the funds are restricted in use, surely schools with billions of dollars can do more in terms of grants and scholarships.

Besides having a work-study job, starting a part-time business, especially one that can generate recurring cash flow, is a great way to reduce the weight of student debt. We address entrepreneurship in Chapter Four.

Positive Peers

Another obstacle is the mentality of some of the high school students. Many students simply have no frame of reference in that they know few, if any, other students who attended college. Some students are part of peer groups that discourage them from working hard to obtain a higher education. When I was in high school, I wore thick unfashionable glasses because I could not afford designer frames or contact lenses for my severe nearsightedness. I guess I looked like an egghead or nerd in those glasses. I was teased about my grades weekly, with the verbal shots often coming from other African American students. Academically, I never wavered in my commitment to higher education. However, socially, I realized by 12th grade that it was time for me to find a new peer group and playing field where my skill set might be more widely appreciated. I wanted to meet some college friends who would value my focus on education.

My own son, Joshua, has been more fortunate in terms of having an encouraging peer group. Outside of school, he spent four years actively participating in the Leaders of Tomorrow (LOT) High School Mentoring Program in Houston, Texas. They have monthly workshops that the National Black MBA Association facilitates to prepare students for leadership in the workforce and in their communities. Case in point, through teamwork and a lot of hard work, he and his colleagues earned 2nd Place in the 2019 MBA Business Case Competition in Houston.

It is important that parents set high expectations for their children. My son *always* knew he was going to college. As parents, we talked about it with him regularly for as long as we can remember. It was just a matter of him figuring out a major to study and which college to attend.

Cultural expectations also matter. Even though I grew up in a disadvantaged background, fortunately, in school, I was always in the college prep classroom – the so-called "smart group". This was based on standardized test scores from, at least, as early as 5th grade. In the culture of that college prep classroom, almost everyone had the expectation of one day getting a university education. The mindset of those peers had a positive impact on me during middle school. Middle school definitely matters, especially in terms of setting up the student for advanced courses in high school.

My son went to a very highly ranked public school. Surviving the rigorous standards at his high school definitely prepared him for college and the SAT test. We live in an upper-middle-class neighborhood. Our son now understands that his dad bought the house in this specific neighborhood so that he could attend elite public schools for his K-12 education. Thus, the fact that his parents are homeowners in our specific neighborhood will help our son go to the college of his choice and have an excellent shot at the American Dream. Unfortunately, everyone does not have those advantages. While students can often make it to college from any neighborhood, it is really nice for them to have a leg up compared to their peers. Because of the demanding K-12 curriculum at our neighborhood schools, my son earned a stellar SAT score. This was a big factor in him getting accepted into his first-choice university.

As a society, to help our next generation of rising stars, conversations and relationships must be encouraged to capture the student's attention before any culture of low expectations sets in. Too many kids are still impacted negatively by living in the "wrong zip code" in America, and we all know there are many brilliant kids that could thrive if they had opportunities to see and do a little more.

Life Lesson:

To help our next generation of rising stars, conversations must be encouraged to capture the student's attention before any culture of low expectations sets in.

The bottom line is to surround yourself with people who have similar positive academic and career goals.

Connection to Community

Another obstacle is that some students do not feel connected to their communities. And lacking that connection, they may feel isolated and sometimes struggle, or at least underachieve academically. This happened to me when I was in 5th grade, as my mother moved us from inner-city Pittsburgh, about 25 miles, to a predominantly white, working-class town called New Brighton. I struggled for more than a year, adjusting to being one of the few African American children in the school. I was not living up to my academic potential.

Even with this or other potential disconnects, young people can find many ways to get involved in the community, especially through service. Students can volunteer in soup kitchens or homeless shelters. They can tutor younger kids, especially those with developmental disabilities. Students who care about the future of the planet can volunteer on an environmental or recycling project. Volunteering builds character and interpersonal skills that are valuable in your career and complement your education.

Participating in sports was critical to my personal adjustment to living in New Brighton. Sports are extremely important in western Pennsylvania, and my success in sports as a New Brighton Lion made me an accepted member of the scholastic community. Sensing this general acceptance, I overcame the occasional encounters with prejudice. The first year I played on the football team, 7th grade, was the first year I earned a 4.0 GPA on every report card. I learned that sports had the potential to provide a way to pay for college and that sports provided skills that carried over to other parts of my life. For example, sports taught me how to be a part of a team, be responsible, set goals, and be healthy and physically fit. I also learned to be a leader, to take direction from a manager or coach, and to win graciously. Sports build *willpower* that can be applied elsewhere – the 8-year-old kids that diligently practice dribbling a soccer ball or basketball for hours on end often eventually become the 8th graders who can start and finish their homework on time.

Most of all, sports taught me how to learn from defeat and bounce back stronger the next time. Consider participation in sports in high school and college as a way to enhance your connection to the campus community and your professional development.

To put it concisely, from high school to graduate school to your Ph.D. program, you need to be connected to your academic community and the larger community around you.

In America, we spend hundreds of billions of dollars per year on education. Improving education involves some complex issues with multiple stakeholders. At the risk of simplifying the challenges, I have some quick takes on public policy ideas we can consider.

One challenge for many families is access to test prep services that can help students excel on standardized tests, such as the SAT and ACT. Public policy could be put in place so that quality prep services can be free for students whose families make less than $70,000 or so per year, combined. This ensures that students of all socioeconomic backgrounds have the opportunity to excel, which is critical for our nation's future growth. Some localities have resources to help, but we need a coherent national focus on this to invest in America's future.

Another concept that deserves more consideration is attempting to improve education, especially in underserved areas, by implementing school vouchers. *But let me be very clear;* I do not support school vouchers that allow public money to be diverted to private schools. Public tax dollars getting diverted to religious-based private schools does not sound like a separation of church and state to me.

The voucher concept I would support would be limited to public schools only in a given city or county, or school district. This way, public schools are forced to compete with each other, and the ones that excel get rewarded for demonstrating the desired behaviors. The rewards would include a larger budget for the school to spend and better pay for teachers and administrators. Schools and their students would be measured based on items, such as grades, attendance, graduation rates, performance on state and national standardized tests, etc. Private schools should always be an option for individuals who can afford it, but public tax dollars should not be used for private schools, in my opinion. By the way, the Thomas Brooks of the 1970s on the North Side of Pittsburgh could not have afforded private school, even with vouchers covering a big chunk of the cost.

In general, I like school choice options for students within public school districts that allow the parent to enroll the child at other schools in the same district. Other schools might offer a program or opportunity that is not available at the home school. Dual credit and advanced placement options are often available for students that are either willing or persuaded by parents to enroll. Such classes are difficult and rigorous, but the students can thrive, assuming proper support and training for staff, students, and parents.

Implementation would not be easy. Safeguards would have to be put in place to prevent administrators from "cherry-picking" the data from the various campuses. However, strengthening public schools with competition and vouchers could be part of the answer.

Finally, we need public schools to offer students more opportunities to learn how to become entrepreneurs and investors. Most public schools condition students for corporate America, not for entrepreneurship. As a result, it falls on the parents to teach their kids about investing and business ownership – and many parents do not have the mindset or the ability to do that successfully. We cover entrepreneurship in Chapter Four of this book.

In summary, there are opportunities and there are challenges as we develop the next generation of young professionals and entrepreneurs. As President Barack Obama said, *"If you think education is expensive, wait until you see how much ignorance costs in the 21st century."*

My advice to you is to surround yourself with people who have similar educational and career goals. Then, *work extremely hard* to achieve academically and consider getting not only a bachelor's degree but also a master's degree in a field congruent with your passion – as an enabler to finding a career or an entrepreneurial path that generates enjoyment and long-term recurring cash flow.

> **Life Lesson:**
>
> Surround yourself with people who have similar educational and career goals. Then, work extremely hard to achieve academically.

Remember that education is a life-long journey and not limited to just the classroom. For many, formal instruction can get you a job, but self-education can make you wealthy.

> *"A system of education is not one thing, nor does it have a single definite object, nor is it a mere matter of schools. Education is that whole system of human training within and without the schoolhouse walls, which molds and develops men."*
>
> — W. E. B. Du Bois, civil rights activist, historian, and author

#DoItNow – What Actions Will You Take as a Result of Reading This Chapter?
1)
2)
3)

CHAPTER FOUR

ENTREPRENEURIAL MINDSET

"Profits are better than wages. Wages will make you a living, profits can make you a fortune."

— Jim Rohn, entrepreneur, author
and motivational speaker

Small businesses are so important to the American economy. According to the Small Business Administration, there are an estimated 30 million small businesses in our country and about 8 million of them are owned by people of color. Overall, U.S. small businesses employ over 58 million people, which is nearly half of the country's private workforce. Therefore, for our own sustainability, we must support local small businesses whenever possible.

By the time he began middle school, my son, Joshua, had decided that he was going to start his own business one day. He had watched his parents patronize local small businesses – restaurants, plumbers, landscapers, auto mechanics, etc., and he could see the passion that each of these owners has for their businesses. They seemed to be driven and resilient. His parents also seemed to be more comfortable doing business with local establishments as opposed to national chains. He is now committed to the plan of owning his own business by the time he finishes graduate school.

To achieve their career and financial goals, young people must be more creative than ever before to pay for their education instead of just relying on student loans. Furthermore, as young professionals, they will need to exercise responsible and sound judgment related to spending, budgeting, and credit cards. This will allow them to save money and leverage credit, thereby putting themselves in a prime position to open a small business.

Having a part-time business – especially one that can generate a recurring income – is a great way to reduce the crushing burden of student debt. Besides the money, having a part-time business while you are young can help hone your entrepreneurial mindset. Even in an economic downturn, like the one we face now in 2020-2021, there is never a terrible time to launch a small business.

> **Life Lesson:**
>
> Having a part-time business – especially one that can generate a recurring income – is a great way to reduce the crushing burden of student debt.

There are generally five different things you can do with your money: spend it, save it, invest it, give it away, and pay taxes.

Spending and saving are generally understood. Having an entrepreneurial mindset requires that you spend wisely and try to be frugal. You do not want to be an impulsive buyer. You should minimize (and eventually eliminate) debt, including credit cards, unless you are using the debt to obtain an asset that may potentially appreciate, such as real estate investment properties. Learn to pay yourself first by saving and investing before taking care of your other monthly financial obligations. Payroll deduction of the money you want to save is a great way to go. The money can go directly into a 401(k) plan or IRA before you get a chance to touch it. Remember that a salary is nice, but net worth – and having your money work for you – is far more important.

On your way to becoming an entrepreneur, it is also important to have an emergency savings. For most people, there are unexpected car repairs, healthcare issues, or untimely family obligations. Since we know these things will often happen, we must have an emergency savings to deal with them. In short, most Americans can use some more financial education to protect themselves. It is typically not taught in high school or college.

However, when it comes to financial education, we can learn from one of the principles of Robert Kiyosaki, author of *Rich Dad, Poor Dad*. Specifically, that you want to move from being an employee or self-employed (e.g., a doctor with her own office) toward being a business owner or an investor. The idea is to create leverage. Most people start their careers working for money, but eventually, you want to get to the point where your cash-flowing assets pay for your monthly expenses. This gives you a measure of financial freedom.

Most people never begin investing – not due to lack of capital or motivation – due to their fears of making a mistake. A fun way to "practice" investing is by playing Kiyosaki's CASHFLOW game. This allows you to learn how to buy and sell stocks and real estate by doing it the same way you learn to ride a bike. Whether you lose or win, you will learn every time how to build cash-flowing assets or passive income so that you can get out of the rat race. In most cities or towns, there is one or several informal groups that get together to play the game. You can sign up at no cost on Meetup.com and then search for CASHFLOW game events in your area. I host a monthly event in Houston. You can even play anytime online for free.

Over the last 100 years, investing in stocks, real estate, and owning businesses has proven to be far more profitable over the long term than just putting your money in a savings account. Invest for the long term. The key is that you must be able to tolerate the risk of stock market fluctuations and the risks of businesses that have good years and bad years, realizing that the longer you hold on to them, the more they *generally* will increase in value. Anything worth having in business comes with risks. There are no guarantees; thus, you may fail. You may fail again, but your perseverance will pay off. Stay the course. Ignore the naysayers and continue to believe in yourself. You will be your biggest supporter.

Paying taxes is something you cannot avoid. Small and midsize business owners, as opposed to traditional employees, get many more tax deductions because of the expenses of running a company. Rightly or wrongly, the tax system in our country favors homeowners and business owners. A savvy business owner takes advantage of all available legal deductions. Consult a tax professional for assistance. One of the best parts of being a business owner – especially while you are young – is that you can use these deductions. Also, if you give to charities to support important causes in your community, you can deduct those donations from your taxes, as well.

Life Lesson:

Small business owners get many more tax deductions. Rightly or wrongly, the tax system in our country favors homeowners and business owners.

Some people have momentary dreams of entrepreneurship. However, they often come back to their desire for perceived 'security' with their job at a private company or a government agency. At this point, we should all know that a job where you work for someone else is not a guarantee of income due to layoffs, company closures, and government shutdowns.

A case in point, remember the U.S. federal government shut down from December 22, 2018, until January 25, 2019 – a total of 35 painful days. Even if you were not a government employee, you were impacted if your company had any government contracts. When you combine 800,000 federal government employees and some 4 million federal contractors, that shutdown directly affected nearly 3% of the labor force of the United States. Plus, with our nation so politically divided these days, any future shutdowns could be much longer. And with the economy severely impacted by the COVID-19 pandemic in 2020-2021, we know that jobs in corporate America cannot be considered secure. Entrepreneurship is not easy. Sacrifice and delayed gratification will be required. However, owning your own business gives you more control of your destiny over the long-term.

Let me clarify. Some people have great careers in corporate America. If someone is not willing or able to develop their entrepreneurial mindset, then corporate America can be a good place to be. I spent over 20 years in corporate America, and my experience was positive, by and large. However, eventually – even if you are successful in your career in corporate America – I would encourage you to develop a proactive ownership mentality. One of the best ways to be financially successful is to own your own destiny. You want to own your own business, even if it is just part-time. Eventually, you want to become an investor by owning rental properties and stocks, thereby having your money work for you. When you do those things, financial success and financial freedom become far more likely.

So, how do you overcome the lure of the *perceived* security of corporate America? Let's examine some things that may be constraining us.

When we say that someone is "out on a limb," this means they are in a dangerous or vulnerable position, where they are not supported by anyone or anything else. This phrase originated from the practice of people climbing trees and the consequence of people putting too much weight on a high, thin branch or limb. Birds never worry about being out on a limb. The reason is their belief. It's not that the birds have faith in the branch. The belief is based on their confidence in their own ability to fly. As an entrepreneur, you must systematically develop belief and confidence in your own abilities.

People often say, "You have to get *out* of your comfort zone." However, that does not usually work. I would submit that one of the best ways to bolster your entrepreneurial mindset is to *expand* your comfort zone, day-by-day, inch-by-inch.

Life Lesson:

One of the best ways to bolster your entrepreneurial mindset is to expand your comfort zone, day-by-day, inch-by-inch.

Most people choose comfort over perceived risk. We are then left with the life we currently have, and for many people, that is not pretty. The "Comfort Zone" will control us until we choose to control it.

American writer, Peter McWilliams, penned, "When we do something new, something different, we push against the parameters of our comfort zone. If we do the new thing often enough, we overcome the fear, guilt, unworthiness, hurt feelings, and anger – and our comfort zone expands. If we back off and honor the "need" to be comfortable, our comfort zone shrinks. It's a dynamic, living thing – always expanding or contracting."

Imagine those same potentially negative emotions – fear, guilt, unworthiness, hurt feelings, and anger – of the Comfort Zone that often constrain us. Imagine those emotions are trapping you inside a tall five-sided fence.

From author Marcel Proust, "The real voyage of discovery consists not in seeking new lands but in seeing with new eyes." Thus, we need to have a new perspective to deal with these emotions.

We can attribute any feeling to a thought that we want, and we can use that truth to dramatically expand this five-sided fence before it traps us into a life we do not wish to lead. Let's break down these five potentially negative emotions to see how we can flip the script on each one:

- **Fear** can be positive, and it is probably the most powerful motivator of all. Fear gives us massive amounts of energy and makes us alert. Thus, we should be grateful for fear. When you are fearful, your motivation is strong and clear. Your attention does not get diverted to unimportant things. Fear can give us a new perspective so we can act *now* in pursuit of our major goals.

- **Hurt feelings** can be a positive tool, especially if you try a new perspective. Recognize that you must actually be concerned if you have hurt feelings. For example, let's say you want to use a Network Marketing business as an entrepreneurial opportunity to achieve financial freedom or for your kids to go across the stage at college graduation, 100% debt-free. If you get a "NO" from a potential recruit or customer, remind yourself that you only have hurt feelings because you deeply care about your kids graduating without any student loans. You can also remind yourself that your friends are not rejecting you; they just do not see your business as a match for their own needs right now. We can still love our friends while focusing on our business success. Keep a journal of your hurt feelings and how you subsequently leveraged a new perspective about those feelings to help your business or personal life.

- **Anger** can be a powerful positive tool that can increase creativity and performance when focused and targeted correctly. Consider a new perspective that anger can accelerate your progress toward your goals. The optimal way to muzzle your haters or anyone that makes you angry is to stand out in what you do. The excellent results will speak for themselves. If you are angry, get yours by taking positive action and being successful.

- **Guilt** is energy, and most people are using it wrongly. Guilt needs to be directed to accomplish something. When you feel guilty about not completing some task to advance toward a major goal, don't sweat it. Consider a new perspective that the guilt means that you have the knowledge and ability to achieve the goal. You would not feel guilty otherwise. Eradicate the fear that is in the way. Ralph Waldo Emerson taught us to take action, *"Do the thing you fear and the death of fear is certain."*

- **Feeling unworthy** can be a positive tool. Consider a new perspective that you actually are worthy, so you can have pretty much whatever you want. But there is a limitation. As Oprah Winfrey said, *"You can have it all. Just not all at once."* You are no longer a child who wants to be a dancer, pro athlete, schoolteacher, astronaut, and fireman. You must choose based on current priorities. Do you want to be an entrepreneur, caregiver for your elderly parents, youth soccer coach, a triathlete, AND run a high school mentoring program? If you have no priorities and focus, you will fail, and it will lead to – you guessed it – feelings of unworthiness.

Make a choice to use these five emotions as positive tools instead of things that hold you back. It takes determination and practice. This is how we can overcome the lure of the perceived security of corporate America. And you can begin as an entrepreneur on a *part-time* basis while you are still in corporate America. You do not have to be a full-time entrepreneur right away. Author and entrepreneur, Dr. George C. Fraser, taught us, "Don't work eight hours for a company and then go home and not work on your own goals. You're not tired, you're uninspired."

Life Lesson:

Make a choice to use these five emotions as positive tools instead of things that hold you back. It takes determination and practice.

Now that you are aware that the five components can be positive, you will want to *expand* your Comfort Zone, day-by-day, just a few inches at a time, and soon you will be developing your entrepreneurial mindset and accomplishing your major goals.

Entrepreneurs of today have an incredible advantage compared to those of the 1980s. We can leverage the Internet to develop a business and reach customers. Also, the Internet is always on, which gives us a potential opportunity to efficiently work for three to five hours after dinner, even while successfully holding down a day job. And more entrepreneurial time can be invested on the weekends.

Every entrepreneur knows that the customer experience is impacted by more factors than the experience you have in the store. The customer experience is also influenced by how a customer interacts with your technology - your website, mobile application, social media pages, and online review sites. Customers – for any major purchase – typically research your product or service online before buying. Review sites, such as Yelp, have a major influence, and that will only increase in the future. Your brand can be made -- or ruined -- on social media. These strong trends will continue, so it will be up to business owners to adapt or die.

Traditional marketing is customarily what most people are exposed to daily, which includes print ads in newspapers and magazines, TV commercials, telemarketing, and direct mail. Every high school student who takes a class in business or marketing knows about the 4 Ps of marketing – Product, Price, Place, and Promotion.

Internet marketing is similar in that the same 4 Ps are very important. However, Internet marketing does not have all the problems of traditional marketing. Traditional marketing is very costly, especially for TV ads, and you cannot really determine if it is working. Thus, it's hard to measure return on investment (ROI). There is also no real connection to your audience through traditional marketing methods.

From now on, individuals and businesses will build their brand with Gen Z consumers primarily through Internet marketing, including websites, blogs, vlogs, emails, online ads, and social media.

How can one manage the increased competition and other complexities that an online marketplace produces? Internet marketing has some advantages in that most people do some level of research online before buying a product. Also, most adults with spending power are using social media sites, such as Facebook, Instagram, and Twitter on a regular or even daily basis. If you do online ads, the results are easily measurable. And you can easily change or replace an online ad that is not working and then measure those results. A strong online presence can also help you build a following or create a community, allowing you to outflank your competition. You can generate a buzz about your product or even enhance the brand of an individual. In short, Internet marketing is a great way to get leverage and kickstart your entrepreneurial dreams, even if you are doing just part-time.

Regardless of your specialty, look to get started as an entrepreneur, at least part-time. Step into your greatness. If you need help launching your entrepreneurial dreams, contact me at AlphaMultimedia.com. Do not wait since the timing will never be perfect. Just do it now!

> "To live in a system of free enterprise, and to not understand the rules of free enterprise – must be the very definition of slavery."
>
> — Ambassador Andrew Young, civil rights icon, former Mayor of Atlanta

#DoItNow – What Actions Will You Take as a Result of Reading This Chapter?
1)
2)
3)

CHAPTER FIVE

SELF-DISCIPLINE
EQUALS FREEDOM

"We all have dreams. But in order to make dreams come into reality, it takes an awful lot of determination, dedication, self-discipline, and effort."

— Jesse Owens, four-time Olympic gold medalist

For everything you eventually will achieve, expect training, discipline, and hard work along the way. To be a great leader in a specific field, you must have self-discipline. You cannot ascend to great heights without self-discipline. Self-discipline is the required connection between good intentions and great results.

I think of self-discipline as getting myself to do things I must do when I need to get them done, even if I really *do not feel like* doing it. Candidly, when it comes to achievement, your "feelings" do not matter. What matters are the goals you are committed to and the related actions you take. Let your actions lead your feelings. You will get the task done, and then you will "feel" better in the end. Make sure you drive your behaviors and movements to control your thoughts. For example, sometimes, after a long and busy day, I have it in my schedule to go work out. However, in some cases, I may not "feel" like going to the gym. If I get to the gym and complete the workout, I always "feel" great. You will want to learn to conquer your emotions through the habit of taking positive action. We shall cover habits later in this chapter.

Life Lesson:

When it comes to achievement, your "feelings" do not matter. What matters are the goals you are committed to, and the related actions you take.

Self-discipline and freedom, on the surface, may seem to oppose each other. However, in reality, self-discipline is the enabler of freedom.

There are many definitions of freedom that you may want to pursue. Some people have a deep desire for financial freedom, which gives you security and a lot of options. Others focus on time freedom, having the autonomy to do what they want, whenever they want. A soul mate gives us the freedom to feel and enjoy love. Some people want location freedom, to live where they want or to travel where they want. Other people yearn for creative freedom. Those who value contribution and legacy – like General Benjamin O. Davis, Jr., who will be discussed later in this chapter – long for giving freedom.

What does freedom look like to you? What is it that you really want?

In Chapter Two, we covered the concept of your Definite Major Purpose (DMP) and focusing on that overarching goal – your *primary goal* for which you have a burning desire. It takes self-discipline.

Related to self-discipline is the concept of *delayed gratification*. We often see this in play with young people whose Definite Major Purpose is to become a doctor. Many aspiring doctors take on challenging undergraduate majors, such as Chemistry, Biology, or Biomedical Engineering. Eventually, some of these aspirants decide that they do not feel like having such a demanding major. So, they change majors and subsequently choose to give up on their primary goal.

Other students stick with their demanding major and earn their Bachelor of Science degree. However, they decide to get started working immediately after graduation – making money now instead of going through four years of medical school and another three years, at minimum, for a residency. Note that some doctors do additional fellowships that take even longer. Those students who choose to start working right after getting their bachelor's degree have given up on their primary goal – at least, at that moment in life.

To hang in there for the additional seven or more years while piling up student loan debt takes some serious delayed gratification. Especially since while you are in medical school, many of your friends by their mid-twenties are already established in their careers, earning money, driving fast cars, and having a lot of free time to spend with the people they care about.

However, eventually, if one keeps their eyes on the prize, the doctor finishes their education and training and can then enjoy a rewarding career based on solving problems, helping people, and saving lives. And the money at the end of your medical training is typically rather good, as well. As mentioned previously, one type of freedom is financial freedom. Those doctors who finished their training did what they needed to do, even though they did not always feel like doing it. That self-discipline allowed them to reach their primary goal. Self-discipline can equate to freedom.

Most people would like to eventually get to a point in life where they have time freedom or financial freedom. Self-discipline boils down to not giving up on the things you want most out of life in exchange for something you feel that you desire right now.

Life Lesson:

Self-discipline boils down to not giving up on the things you want most out of life in exchange for something you feel that you desire right now.

Self-discipline — more so than where you start out socioeconomically or your IQ or many other factors — generally has the most to do with your long-term wealth creation. Self-discipline can help you develop the habit of being frugal, dedicated to spending less and saving more. Self-discipline can help you develop the habit of proper planning for your financial future. When you have self-discipline, you have the habit of learning what you need to know in relation to money, investing, and wealth.

How do we become more disciplined? Some of us are stuck in bad habits. Please understand that only a new habit can overpower the bad habit, and it will take consistency and persistent repetition of the new habit. After a period of repetition, you become good at the new habit or task. Of course, you will get enjoyment from doing it once you are good at it, creating a new, positive cycle of self-discipline related to the good habit you want to maintain.

A key component of success in replacing old habits with better habits is *belief.* You must believe that there is a brighter future ahead. Belief is more easily developed when you are part of a group. For example, if you are trying to give up alcohol, you will likely have a stronger belief that it is possible if you consistently attend the local Alcoholics Anonymous meetings. A similar dynamic happens with underdog sports teams who suddenly start believing in each other and in their collective ability to win a championship.

Once you are disciplined in terms of a task or habit, how do you maintain it? I had a sign on my wall as an undergraduate student at the University of Pittsburgh. The sign read, 'Prioritize Unpleasant Tasks First.' So, yes, I sometimes missed out on fun as I pursued my Electrical Engineering degree. However, having that sign gave me daily motivation to keep on hustling to get my degree and lift myself out of poverty. A visual cue helps reinforce good habits and keeps important things from falling through the cracks. And often, I was able to finish the unpleasant task first – such as my homework in Differential Calculus – and then still go out later and have a good time. Achievement is not a random occurrence. You must be purposeful, exercising perseverance in pursuit of perfection, and that takes discipline.

To prove these principles, Pulitzer Prize-winning writer, Charles Duhigg, performed extensive research on habits, which he shares in his book, *The Power of Habit.*

Every habit has three components: a reminder that serves as a *cue* or trigger, a *routine* that is the behavior itself, and the *reward* that gets you to repeat the behavior again and again. Duhigg calls this 'The

Habit Loop', and it is the cue and the reward that determines how habits function. When you feel trapped in a bad habit, the reward for that bad habit is often the part that is difficult to isolate. The reward may be a subconscious feeling.

Life Lesson:

Every habit has three components: a reminder that serves as a cue or trigger, a routine that is the behavior itself, and the reward that gives you incentive.

How can you increase willpower? You do it by changing habits. Willpower is a skill that can be learned and improved upon, according to Duhigg's research. You teach people to make a specific decision ahead of time and teach them to apply that decision when they get the cue or trigger, and then you reward them. By premeditating the specific cues and rewards, you can change any habit in your life.

For example, if you want to work out every morning, put your running shoes right by the bed. The running shoes serve as the cue. If you want to gain more knowledge, as you are grabbing breakfast or coffee and heading out to work, start up your audiobook app on your phone to make great use of your morning commute. Tying it to something – a cue – that is *already* part of your daily routine (grabbing breakfast or coffee) is more effective than just randomly inserting the audiobook into your day.

If you want to make 15 sales calls per day to achieve your goals, move one quarter from a glass on your left and place in another glass on the other side of your desk each time you make a call. Once you have, at least, 15 quarters on the right, give yourself some reward, which can be tangible or intangible. If you are on the go, you can use dimes – they are lighter – and your front pockets, instead of the two glasses.

Duhigg tells the story of a previous experiment that was done to measure willpower in the 1960s called the Marshmallow Test. That researcher put a marshmallow in front of his daughter and did the same with a group of other four-year-old children at her school. The children were each told that if they can resist eating the marshmallow for 10 minutes, they will be given a second marshmallow. Only 10% to 15% of the kids could resist the marshmallow.

When his daughter reached 5th grade, the researcher looked at how the kids were doing. He gathered data on how the original children performed as teens and after college as young adults, and it turned out that the kids who could resist the marshmallow tended to do better socially and academically. The kids with the willpower were more popular in high school. They got into better colleges and got better-paying jobs.

Willpower and self-discipline are related. Think of willpower as a temporary surge of focus. Self-discipline is more long term and dependable. Self-discipline is sparked by *desire* – the type of burning desire you have for your DMP or primary goal. For example, if you want to lose weight, willpower could help you ignore the big plate of cookies your co-worker placed in the break area for everyone. Self-discipline enables you to ignore unhealthy food on a daily basis.

When it comes to habits, I take inspiration from some words from a leadership guru, John Maxwell:

Everything worthwhile is an uphill climb. You don't reach your dream by sliding downhill. It takes self-discipline to climb every day. The problem is we have uphill hopes and downhill habits.

While there are other important variables, such as support, education, and socioeconomic advantages, you must have self-discipline. You cannot expect to coast to achievement. Self-discipline enables freedom.

If you want to get in shape, you must exercise since calories will not burn themselves. If you want to be an author, the book will not write itself. If you have a Network Marketing business, the Associates or Distributors for your team will not recruit themselves. If you want to plan a two-week vacation on another continent, the travel funds will not accumulate by themselves. I could rattle off twenty more examples, but you get the point. Think carefully about what habits you must develop to reach your primary goal and the cue, routine, and reward necessary to make the new habits work for you.

> **Life Lesson:**
> Think carefully about what habits you must develop to reach your primary goal, and the cue, routine, and reward necessary to make the new habits work for you.

Jim Rohn taught, "Everyone must choose one of two pains: The pain of discipline or the pain of regret." A brilliant and inspirational example of discipline without career regrets is the Tuskegee Airmen, and specifically their squad leader, Benjamin O. Davis, Jr.

Davis often faced bigotry, discrimination, and racial prejudice. He began his stellar career at the US Military Academy at West Point in 1932. Davis roomed alone for four years and was only addressed by his peers on matters of official business. He had no social interaction with other future Army officers and was "silenced" by the Corps of Cadets, the harshest treatment given out by the student body – reserved for those that violate the Honor Code. Of course, his only transgression was that he was African American, but his self-discipline would not allow him to quit.

Despite the abuse, Davis graduated in 1936 with an excellent class ranking – 35th out of a class of 276. Though he wanted to fly and join the Army Air Corp, he was not allowed because of his skin color. He subsequently joined the 24th Infantry Regiment at Fort Benning, Georgia. As a manifestation of his discipline, Davis was promoted to First Lieutenant ahead of schedule. He was eventually assigned to Tuskegee University as a Professor of Military Science.

According to his Air Force biography, after America's entry into World War II, Davis transferred to the Army Air Corps in May 1942. As commander of the all-black 99th Fighter Squadron at Tuskegee, he moved with his unit to North Africa in April 1943 and later to Sicily. He returned to the United States in October 1943, assumed command of the 332nd Fighter Group at Selfridge Field, Michigan, and returned with that group to Italy two months later. His disciplined leadership played a key role in the success of the legendary Tuskegee Airmen. Under the leadership of Colonel Davis, the 332nd escorted American bombers in missions over the Mediterranean and central Europe. During the war, the squadron – known as the *Red Tails* for the unique markings of its planes – compiled an outstanding record in combat against the Luftwaffe, the name the Nazis give to their air forces. They flew more than 15,000 sorties, shot down 112 German Luftwaffe planes, and destroyed or damaged 273 on the ground. The Tuskegee Airmen also did an excellent job of escorting American bombers.

Despite the impact of Jim Crow, both inside and outside the military, Davis stayed disciplined and persevered. In July 1948, President Harry Truman signed an Executive Order for the racial integration of the armed forces. Davis helped draft the Air Force plan for implementing this order. The Air Force was the first of the services to integrate fully. Davis was eventually promoted in 1954 to be the first black brigadier general in the U.S. Air Force. He was a barrier breaker because of his discipline.

In 1998, President Bill Clinton honored Davis at the White House, saying, "Today, we advance to the rank of four-star General Benjamin O. Davis, Jr.; a hero in war, a leader in peace, a pioneer for freedom, opportunity, and basic human dignity. He earned this honor a long time ago. Our Armed Forces today are a model for America and for the world of how people of different backgrounds working together for the common good can perform at a far more outstanding level than they ever could divided."

For this outstanding American general, who valued contribution and legacy, obtaining *giving freedom* was important – and he achieved it through his military service. Self-discipline equals freedom. Think about the barriers you can crash through as you hone your self-discipline and develop new habits.

Dr. Stephen Covey told the story of an instructor who stood in front of a group of students. The instructor said, "Okay, time for a quiz." Then he pulled out a one-gallon, wide-mouthed mason jar and set it on a table in front of him. Then he produced about a dozen fist-sized rocks and carefully placed them, one at a time, into the jar.

When the jar was filled to the top, and no more big rocks would fit inside, he asked, "Is this jar full?" Everyone in the class said, "Yes." Then he said, "Really?" He reached under the table and pulled out a bucket of gravel. Then he dumped some gravel in and shook the jar, causing pieces of gravel to work themselves down into the spaces between the big rocks.

Then he smiled and asked the group once more, "Is the jar full?" By this time, the class was onto him. "Probably not," one of them answered. "Good!" he replied. And he reached under the table and brought out a bucket of sand. He started dumping the sand in, and it went into all the spaces left between the rocks and the gravel. Once more he asked the question, "Is this jar full?"

"No!" the class shouted. Once again, he said, "Good!" Then he grabbed a pitcher of water and began to pour it in until the jar was filled to the brim. Then he looked up at the class and asked, "What is the point of this illustration?"

One student raised his hand and said, "The point is, no matter how full your schedule is, if you try really hard, you can always fit some more things into it."

"No," the speaker replied, "that's not the point. The truth this illustration teaches us is: If you don't put the big rocks in first, you'll never get them in at all."

You must decide what the 'big rocks' are in your life. Pick one or two, but no more than four things – your important goals – and make sure you fit those things in, come hell or high water. That takes discipline because, in the 21st Century, there is always another 'shiny object' to distract you from your top priorities. And, of those important goals, there is no big rock that should be a higher priority than your own Definite Major Purpose (DMP) – your primary goal, the thing you deeply crave.

There is a connection between self-discipline and your DMP. A lack of self-discipline is often caused by a lack of knowing what you *really* want. Your DMP sparks motivation and, as Albert Einstein declared, *"When a man is sufficiently motivated, discipline will take care of itself."*

So, we come back to the questions from the beginning of the chapter – What does freedom look like to you? What is it that you really want?

You can have financial freedom, time freedom, and the freedom to feel and enjoy love. You can have location freedom, creative freedom, or - like General Benjamin O. Davis Jr. - you can obtain giving freedom.

You can have virtually anything or any freedom you crave with the self-discipline created with positive, focused habits. Self-discipline equals freedom.

"I don't count my sit-ups; I only start counting when it starts hurting, when I feel pain, that's when I start counting, cause that's when it really counts."

— Muhammad Ali, activist, philanthropist, and 3-time world heavyweight boxing champion

#DoItNow – What Actions Will You Take as a Result of Reading This Chapter?
1)
2)
3)

CHAPTER SIX

YOU AREN'T LEADING IF NO ONE IS FOLLOWING

"Leadership is not about titles, positions or flowcharts. It is about one life influencing another."

— John Maxwell, author, speaker, and pastor

Leadership can be characterized as the art of influencing a group of people to take steps toward accomplishing a common objective. In a business setting, this can mean planning, guiding, and directing colleagues to achieve the desired metrics for the business.

As a John Maxwell Certified Coach, Teacher, Trainer and Speaker, and leader, I have five guiding principles that I live by daily. I believe that we can all put these principles into action to become better leaders:

- Hard Work
- Kindness
- Gratitude
- Enthusiasm
- Competitive Greatness

Let's take a closer look at each of these principles:

Principle One – Hard Work

One of the best ways to lead by example is to work hard. Talent and luck will only get you so far. For example, Michael Jordan won six NBA Championships for the Chicago Bulls. And the sports world could see that he was a gifted player, even while he was in college. In 1982, he hit the game-winning shot in the NCAA Championship Game to seal the victory for the North Carolina Tar Heels. However, it was hard work that really made Jordan a legend and arguably the greatest basketball player of all time. When Jordan was a rookie in the NBA, he was great at driving to the basket and elevating for dunks and easy layups. Eventually, to contain Jordan, teams started collapsing most of their defenders into the painted area near the basket and forced him to take more jump shots. His jump shot still needed to be more consistent, so Jordan practiced taking hundreds of jumpers each day until he improved. He worked on his passing to get the ball to open teammates when he was double-teamed. That was one way he made his teammates better.

Life Lesson:

One of the best ways to lead by example is to work hard. Talent and luck will only get you so far.

Over the years, the other teams began to go after him with rough, aggressive play. Teams like the Detroit Pistons implemented the notorious "Jordan Rules". This style of defense limited players, including Jordan, from entering the painted area by pounding him with brutal physical contact. So, Jordan started spending hours in the weight room to put on muscle – body armor – so that he could survive all the hard fouls. The hard work paid off, and Jordan won seven straight NBA scoring titles from 1986–87 to 1992–93.

As Jordan got older, he lost a bit of his athleticism. So, he added a post-up game with a deadly turnaround jump shot ranging from eight to fifteen feet. By 1998, the year Jordan won his sixth NBA title, Jordan used his fadeaway jump shot to become one of the best post-up players in the league. The technique extended his career. And as a result, Jordan won three additional NBA scoring titles – at the relatively old ages of 33, 34 and 35. Jordan's work ethic is widely admired, and it allowed him to finish his career nearly as strong as he started. Yes, he was sometimes excessively harsh with his teammates, but his teammates could not question his burning desire to win because they saw his strong work ethic daily. That work ethic is what made Jordan an example – and thereby a leader – for his teammates. Players around the league noticed this. Eventually, other players, such as Kobe Bryant, mimicked Jordan's style of leadership by demonstrating a strong work ethic. LeBron James, while still in high school, learned by watching how Jordan made his teammates so much better.

Although he was writing about business, Professor Phil Rosenzweig could have been referring to Jordan when he wrote in Harvard Business Review, *"Only those who are able to muster a degree of commitment and determination that is by some definitions excessive will be in a position to win."*

What can you learn from Jordan's evolution as a player and team leader that can enhance your career or entrepreneurial endeavors?

Principle Two – Kindness

I know it sounds simple but just being nice adds value to people. It can change the world in an instant when you are kind to each person you meet. Think of how the world would change for the better if we all did just one random act of kindness each day.

As leaders, we also must be deliberate about practicing kindness. Random acts are wonderful. However, let's not miss opportunities to be kind *on purpose* to consistently make the team better, raise someone's spirits, and basically look out for our colleagues.

Life Lesson:

Be deliberate about practicing kindness. Random acts of kindness are wonderful. However, let's not miss opportunities to be kind on purpose.

How can we, as leaders, be kind with strategic intention? Recognition is one way. The old saying is, "Recognition: babies cry for it, grown men die for it." Yes, people want raises and promotions in the workplace. However, what they crave – and typically do not get – is public recognition.

Praise is another way to show kindness. Coach Bill Walsh, a 3-time Super Bowl Champion, remarked, "Few things offer greater return on less investment than praise – offering credit to someone in your organization who has stepped up and done the job." When you give that praise, as a leader, you want to be extremely *specific*. Do not just say, "Thanks." Instead, say something like, "Hey, Amy, I really appreciated the detailed data collection and analysis. Thanks for getting the project done before the deadline!"

As leaders, we also want to be kind when giving constructive feedback. Critiquing a team member's performance can be challenging, but a trusting relationship can be created if it is done with kindness and positivity.

And leaders demonstrate kindness by serving others. To paraphrase the great Dr. Martin Luther King, "Everyone can be a great leader because everyone can serve." As a leader, you want to think daily about how you can make things better for the people who are following you. If you do not serve others, soon you will have no followers, and – by definition – you are no longer a leader.

Think about the people you are leading or those you want to lead. How best can you serve their interests?

Principle Three – Gratitude

Every one of us has an obligation to ourselves, our friends, our families, and our business associates to be grateful for the opportunities that we have been given every day. It makes people want to be around you, and it makes people want to assist you in business. I obtained countless customers in my career just by showing gratitude in my daily interactions. So, it makes sense that my favorite holiday is Thanksgiving Day. An attitude of gratitude is contagious all year long and essential for stellar leadership.

72

Life Lesson:

An attitude of gratitude is contagious all year long, and essential for stellar leadership.

According to Robert Emmons, Ph.D., a leading scientific expert on gratitude, systematically cultivating gratitude by keeping a "gratitude journal" for a month can have an enormous positive impact. You can become not only a better leader but a better person through the impact of gratitude on your physical and psychological well-being.

From a physical perspective, gratitude may contribute to a stronger immune system, lower blood pressure, and assist with increased sleep, which makes you feel more refreshed upon waking.

From a psychological perspective, gratitude can lead to the perks of higher levels of positive emotions – joy, optimism, happiness, and pleasure. And from a social perspective, you become more helpful, generous, compassionate, and forgiving.

A leadership position is a demanding role if you are doing it well. These perks derived from gratitude help us thrive both mentally and physically.

Think of a couple of people you know that radiate with gratitude. How does that impact the way they lead others in business or in their personal life?

Principle Four – Enthusiasm

One of my guiding principles is to exhibit enthusiasm. To be successful in the long run, you must love what you do. If you do not radiate enthusiasm about what you are doing, how can you expect anyone else to be excited? When I come to train your organization or speak at your event, you had better believe that I will bring some energy!

Life Lesson:

If you do not radiate enthusiasm about what you are doing, how can you expect anyone else to be excited? What if you decided right now to be 10 times more excited?

In my career, I have come across people who are extremely capable but fail completely. These people fail because of their apathetic approach to a task. In other words, they are gifted, but they are not fervent about their ambitions. Due to this lack of enthusiasm, they do not act – they fail to just do it now. Enthusiasm alone can be the guiding force that can help them get rid of their mediocre mindset.

And that enthusiasm can enable you to have self-belief. Regardless of the field in which you are working as a leader, you will not be successful unless you believe in your mission. A leader with a strong belief in his or her own skills, and enthusiastic belief in their team, is highly likely to be successful. We share more about enthusiasm in Chapter Twenty-Three.

What if, for the next seven days, you made the decision to be *10 times more excited* about everything important that you do? As a leader, what response would you expect from those who follow you?

Principle Five – Competitive Greatness

Legendary basketball coach, John Wooden, who led UCLA to 10 NCAA national championships, emphasized the concept of competitive greatness – in other words, you want to deliver your peak performance when greatness is required. You must be results-oriented. If you love what you do, you should enjoy a challenge. A great leader is convinced that he or she can make a positive impact, even when facing severe headwinds, like the recession related to the COVID-19 pandemic, for example, that could make business growth much more difficult.

Life Lesson:

Emphasize the concept of competitive greatness – in other words, you want to deliver your peak performance when greatness is required.

Champions behave like champions long before they are officially declared champions. Your daily habits pave the way for the desired result. As a Super Bowl Champion Coach, Mike Tomlin, likes to say, "The standard is the standard." In other words, there is one standard. Winning is always the standard by which his Pittsburgh Steelers will be measured. When a star player goes down with an injury, when a referee makes a horrible call, when the weather is dreadful, it's all irrelevant in this adage. The standard for Tomlin's Pittsburgh Steelers apparently never changes, even after games they lost. Just do it now and get the job done so the victory can be won.

Competitive greatness has a cost. You must put in the work daily to climb the mountain of competitive greatness – there is no ski lift that will carry you to the top. There is no way to coast to your important goals.

If you exemplify these five guiding principles, everybody will know that you are a leader. They will know because you will have a following.

Challenge yourself. As a leader, do you put a demand on yourself for competitive greatness? How does your team respond?

"Leadership is hard to define, and good leadership even harder. But if you can get people to follow you to the ends of the earth, you are a great leader."

— Indra Nooyi, former CEO of PepsiCo

#DoItNow – What Actions Will You Take as a Result of Reading This Chapter?
1)
2)
3)

CHAPTER SEVEN

THE ART OF SETTING S.M.A.R.T. GOALS

---

*"The trouble with not having a goal
is that you can spend your life running up
and down the field and never score."*

— Bill Copeland, historian, poet and author

Setting goals is a game of precision. You want to set clear and explicit goals that can be measured. In other words, you want to set SMART goals – which stands for Specific, Measurable, Attainable, Relevant, Timeframe – and put them in writing.

The goal must be **specific**. By that, I am saying that you must be crystal clear to the world – and to your own subconscious mind – about what you will accomplish as part of reaching your goal. Remember, your conscious mind is much less powerful and can only hold one thought at a time, but it is the guardian of the subconscious mind. And you, fortunately, have the power to choose that one thought. On the other hand, our subconscious mind is so powerful. By making a choice to appropriately 'program' our subconscious mind with the precise, detailed *written plan* for our specific goal, we tap into Infinite Power (sometimes called infinite intelligence or Universal Mind). We can accomplish virtually anything, as our subconscious mind works on our goals 24/7, providing creativity and inspiration, even while we sleep. We can ask the Universe for anything. I control my thoughts and direct the work of my subconscious mind.

Any goal absolutely must be **measurable**. How else will you know if you are winning the game? I love playing pickup basketball. However, it gets boring quickly if no one is keeping score. You should identify exactly what you will see, count, and experience when you reach your goal. Your happy *feelings* about your future successful experience will be like fuel to your subconscious mind.

Life Lesson:

Any goal absolutely must be measurable. How else will you know if you are winning the game?

You also need your goals to be **attainable**. For example, it is not realistic for me – now well past my athletic prime – to make it to the National Basketball Association (NBA) as a player. If that were my goal, I would just be setting myself up for failure, based on my capabilities. Set goals that are challenging yet attainable.

To make it all worthwhile, your goals must be **relevant**, totally congruent with your Definite Major Purpose (DMP – as covered in Chapter Two), the *main thing* that you desire out of life. If and when you achieve your goal, how will your business or your life be enhanced? Will this achievement make a significant difference? If you are not crystal clear on how to answer those questions, your goal may not be truly relevant.

Finally, your goals should each have a **timeframe** for completion. This helps keep you accountable. And having a timeframe for completion enables you to break down the goal into the weekly and daily tactics necessary to reach the goal. The daily tactics should be put in your calendar because what doesn't get scheduled will usually not get done. These daily tactics become habits. And when we establish a new habit, which often takes about 30 days, the tactics become easier. See Chapter Five for more on habits and self-discipline.

And make sure you remember to ask yourself, "What am I willing to give up to reach my goal?" There is a price to be paid for anything worthwhile. Maybe to create the time to reach your goal, you give up playing in your local softball league. Maybe to create a healthy lifestyle, you limit your chocolate intake to only once per month.

Life Lesson:

What are you willing to give up to reach your goal? There is a price to be paid for anything worthwhile.

Do not have too many goals. I would suggest three to five big goals. If you have too many goals, no matter how well they are written, you are at risk of losing focus. Add other goals only as you complete the big ones currently on your plate – reaching for higher goals *after* each accomplishment is a great way to get momentum in your life and your business.

Write down your goals and look at the list weekly, or better yet, daily, and make sure you pause to reflect and assess your overall progress at least once per month. Facts on the ground may change, necessitating a modification, or even an acceleration of your list of goals.

Let's look at an example. The majority of Americans drag themselves to a job they no longer like while simultaneously worrying about getting fired. So, on New Year's Eve, many people set a goal or a resolution to achieve time freedom and financial freedom during the subsequent new year.

Do not make "resolutions", and do not only think about your dreams on January 1st. If you want something in any area of life, do not focus on anything else daily except the positive thing or the S.M.A.R.T. goal you want to achieve. Do *not* dwell on any weaknesses or deficiencies that you want to remove from your way of being.

Robin Sharma, one of the world's premier speakers on leadership and personal mastery, puts it this way, "What you focus on grows, what you think about expands, and what you dwell upon determines your destiny."

Can you get out of debt by constantly thinking, 'I need money, I am in huge debt'? Not for long, *and* you are making it harder by thinking about 'need' and 'debt'. You are actually growing the tendency to have situations in your life that create (or attract) more 'need' and 'debt'. You need to focus on being wealthy for life, instead. Focus on the positive side of the situation.

You cannot receive your prize if you continue to focus on what you lack. We reap what we sow, exactly. We must make room for only constructive thoughts, such as success, servant leadership, kindness, wealth, and health. We must use only pleasant language.

When you are in a leadership role, you want to give your attention to the Definite Major Purposes (DMPs) of the folks on your team. When you do that, their success or income grows, and your success or income grows as a result. If we 'think' we are struggling, what we focus on grows in our subconscious mind, and we struggle. If we manage to focus on the progress we are making every day, then our progress accelerates.

Life Lesson:

What we focus on grows in our subconscious mind. If we manage to focus on the progress we are making daily, our progress accelerates.

You need to starve your shortcomings to death. If Laura wants to lose weight, she should not think about "dieting". This is because she will *keep ending up in a situation where she needs to "diet" over and over and over*. Instead, Laura should focus on the virtues of moderation or true health. What we focus on grows.

Finally, you can benefit from having an accountability partner to help you reach your S.M.A.R.T. goal. There are several ways to do this, and you can have multiple accountability partners. You can check in with a mentor, monthly or quarterly, to help you stay on track and on schedule. You can also have a peer, someone chasing the same or a similar goal, that you can check in with briefly each week to encourage one another. You can also 'announce' your S.M.A.R.T. goal to your friends by text or on social media. Once many people know what you need to accomplish, there is a greater incentive to do it now instead of having to make excuses.

Napoleon Hill wrote in *Think and Grow Rich* about infinite intelligence. The idea is that we can tap into the massive creative power of the universe. Some call this force Universal Mind. Others refer to this higher power as God. Hill chose the term infinite intelligence because it is neutral and can be applied to any religion. Infinite intelligence can connect with your subconscious mind, even while you sleep, and can provide you with creativity and inspiration. And infinite intelligence works best with specific S.M.A.R.T. goals, as described here previously, to help you create the winning ideas you need to reach your dreams.

> *"I am lucky that whatever fear I have inside me, my desire to win is always stronger."*
>
> — Serena Williams, tennis legend and winner of 23 Grand Slam singles titles

#DoItNow – What Actions Will You Take as a Result of Reading This Chapter?
1)
2)
3)

CHAPTER EIGHT

THE PLATINUM RULE

"Everybody can be great because anybody can serve. You don't have to have a college degree to serve. You don't have to make your subject and verb agree to serve. You only need a heart full of grace. A soul generated by love."

— Dr. Martin Luther King Jr., Nobel Peace Prize Laureate, civil rights leader, activist, and author

The Golden Rule, as taught by Jesus, Confucius, and many others through the centuries, can be paraphrased as "always treat others as you would like them to treat you." The concept appears in Buddhism, Christianity, Hinduism, Judaism, Taoism, and many other religions. The only challenge with this powerful idea is that, in many cases, you might want something different than what the other person may desire.

Author Dave Kerpen came up with the Platinum Rule – Treat others the way that *they* would like to be treated. Dale Carnegie explained the concept this way:

Personally, I am very fond of strawberries and cream, but I have found that for some strange reason, fish prefer worms. So, when I went fishing, I didn't think about what I wanted. I thought about what they wanted. I didn't bait the hook with strawberries and cream. Rather, I dangled a worm or grasshopper in front of the fish and said: "Wouldn't you like to have that?"

I would think that the same sound thought process would work when fishing for people to influence. The Platinum Rule makes a lot of sense.

Life Lesson:

Platinum Rule – Treat others the way
that they would like to be treated.

At the St. Luke's Hospital Transplant Center in Houston, they have a tradition. After discharge, when your transplant is complete, you get to "Ring Out" as you leave the hospital. My wife, who has a hereditary condition called Polycystic Kidney Disease (PKD), got to ring the bell as she left with her new kidney in December 2017. My wife found a living kidney donor, and we are so grateful for that kind stranger – who is now our good friend – and the willingness of that donor to effectively give the gift of life.

Not everyone may want to donate a kidney, but you can do a random act of kindness each day. You cannot lay claim to your prize if you continue to focus on what is missing from your life. For example, you may want money, but if your mind is focused on poverty and your debts, the money is unlikely to come. What we concentrate on tends to increase and expand. Therefore, we want to focus on the positive side of the situation and do random acts of kindness daily.

We reap what we sow. For example, if you sow kindness, you will receive kindness. The best way to achieve extraordinary performance for yourself is to want and to work toward extraordinary performance for everyone.

Life Lesson:

We reap what we sow. The best way to achieve extraordinary performance for yourself is to want and to work toward extraordinary performance for everyone.

Leveraging the platinum rule, we can sow the seeds of kindness in our one-on-one interactions. And driven by the Platinum Rule, we lead or simply work on larger projects in our community. If you are good at math or any other subject, you can be a tutor. You can mentor someone, either individually or as part of a larger mentoring program. Apply the Platinum Rule to other causes that you care about. You can volunteer to provide computer help to residents of a home for seniors. You can work on or start your own recycling program. And food banks need volunteers all year long, not just during the holiday season.

Just remember, whichever path you choose for your service, to treat others the way they would like to be treated.

The goal of the Platinum Rule is harmony and constructive interactions. You do not have to alter your character. You do not have to roll over and surrender to others. You simply must understand what drives people and recognize your options for dealing with them. This applies in all relationships, both personal and professional.

In the book, *Leading with Kindness*, the authors William F. Baker and Michael O'Malley define key qualities of kind leaders as humility, authenticity, gratitude, integrity, humor, and compassion. If you know someone who personifies these attributes, they probably stand out from other leaders in the organization. These leaders set expectations. They provide candid, yet kind feedback. And these leaders promote growth.

Of course, even if you lead with kindness, sometimes conflict does happen. However, part of being kind is to anticipate and resolve conflict *before* it escalates beyond the point of no return. This involves assuming that the other party has only the best intentions and then listening to the other party before jumping to a conclusion.

In your relationships, dating, and otherwise, think about the other person's wishes. For example, I may feel that affection and physical contact are how couples should show their love. However, if my wife wants to receive quality time as a way for me to show my love to her, I should endeavor to meet her needs the way she wants them met. And the reverse is true, as well.

One of the most critical educational and political issues these days is how best to have a civil conversation in a democratic society. Our collective future depends on our ability to have citizens gather, listen to each other, debate, make up their minds, and determine a course of action.

These days, the divergence of opinions, coupled with the speed and access of the Internet make it more difficult to keep our conversations civil. We are confronted with uncivil conversations every day, from shouting matches to opinionated blog posts to rhetoric-filled political debates. It is the fuel for cable news channels. Furthermore, the uncivil dialogue has spilled over to the floors of the U.S. Senate and House of Representatives, setting an unwelcome example for our children that, far too often, manifests itself in cyberbullying or even physical violence.

Let's look at how we can apply the Platinum Rule – treating others the way they want to be treated – in politics or disagreements with strangers.

We can have conversations or debates with some structure and organization, such as a time limit per speaker on each topic. Everyone gets an opportunity to join the civil discourse until all points are heard. The healthy debate can continue until a consensus is reached or a deal is made. Or worst case, both sides just agree to disagree at that time. Healthy civil discourse means that both sides seek an understanding of the other side, even if the disagreement remains.

Life Lesson:

Healthy civil discourse means that both sides seek an understanding of the other side, even if the disagreement remains.

Also, to follow the Platinum Rule, there must be no personal attacks. The idea is to kick around ideas and concepts when we disagree, not to kick around people. Civil discourse with the Platinum Rule should be mostly about listening.

On that note, a great listening technique I have used in dating relationships also has applications for civil discourse. Reflexive listening means focusing totally on the actual message being expressed by the other party in the debate. It means hearing and comprehending the words of the person who is talking to you. It involves forming rapport by reflecting back the thoughts and feelings that you heard and saw. You're not there to offer an opinion or solution at this point. You're simply there to listen. The other person can then verify that what you are reflecting back is actually what they wanted to originally communicate. Reflexive listening is addressed in more detail, including examples in Chapter Seventeen.

Reflexive listening can help improve our politics. It can also help our relationships with our spouse or significant other. I challenge you to unilaterally practice reflexive listening the next time you are in a heated debate. I can think of no better or more practical way to live by the Platinum Rule.

"The measure of a country's greatness is its ability to retain compassion in times of crisis."

— Thurgood Marshall, lawyer, civil rights activist, and U.S. Supreme Court Justice

#DoItNow – What Actions Will You Take as a Result of Reading This Chapter?

1)

2)

3)

CHAPTER NINE

YOUR NETWORK IS
YOUR NET WORTH

"Networking is more about 'farming' than it is about 'hunting'. It's about cultivating relationships."

— Dr. Ivan Misner, Founder of BNI, the world's largest business networking organization

The most effective and successful business leaders from across the globe are typically clever and skillful at developing relationships. Networking is an essential unwritten rule of achievement in any endeavor.

> **Life Lesson:**
> Networking is an essential unwritten rule of achievement in any endeavor.

Some of us network well in social settings, such as parties but miss opportunities for networking to advance our careers or entrepreneurial endeavors. This chapter gives you a guide to developing mutually beneficial business relationships through networking, which is an indispensable part of wealth creation. I believe that we can all put these principles into action to become better at building valuable connections with people:

- Have a Strategic Plan
- Have a Giving Mindset
- Show Up
- Do Not Be Afraid to Ask
- Be a "Thought Leader"
- Volunteer
- Have a Reason to Follow Up
- Follow Up

Let's take a closer look at each of the eight keys to networking success:

Key 1 - Have a Strategic Plan

Figure out your career or entrepreneurial goals, and then put in place a networking plan and list of desired relationships to make it happen. For example, if you want to be U. S. Surgeon General, start by making a list of politicians, executives at the Center for Disease Control, American Medical Association (AMA) leaders, and even former surgeon generals that you want to meet. As you make progress in your career, continually revise your goals and your list of desired networking contacts. If you have an aggressive goal (e.g., CEO of a Fortune 500 firm, raising $50 million in venture capital), network above your current peer group. Do not take on a snobbish attitude with your current peers but stretch yourself to meet the "high-flyers".

Key 2 – Have a Giving Mindset

Before you begin the execution of your strategic plan, take on a sincere giving mindset. Be ready to give, help, or facilitate. The goal of your networking efforts should not be an immediate gain for yourself. For example, in job searching, do not lead with your resume; set up a 15-minute phone meeting, or better yet, a meeting in person with the hiring manager. The outcome of the meeting may be that the job is not right for you and that you may give the hiring manager a lead for the person that is eventually hired. Now, you have helped two people, the hiring manager and the newly hired employee. You grew your sphere of influence, which will benefit you in the long run.

I learned a valuable lesson from the famous author and motivational speaker, Zig Ziglar, *"You can have everything in life you want if you will just help enough other people get what they want."*

Key 3 - Show Up

You must get out there. Take advantage of receptions and events held by organizations in which you are a member. Better yet, attend functions held by organizations where you can find the high-flyers on your strategic list (see Key #1). Since you must eat anyway, use meals to move relationships forward, as you do when dating. For example, if you are new to your company's marketing department, have lunch with the engineering manager. Or, instead of eating dinner alone, attend a reception that serves hors d'oeuvres to make good use of your valuable time.

When you get there, make sure you are prepared. This means that you not only have a business card, but you also know what you have to offer (Key #2) to the people that you want to meet. Know your approach so that you are confident as you break the ice. Make relevant conversation and then close smoothly without monopolizing the other person's entire evening. Do not leave the conversation without a reason to follow up (Key #7).

> **Life Lesson:**
>
> Know your approach, so that you are confident as you break the ice. Make relevant conversation and then close smoothly without monopolizing their entire evening.

Key 4 - Do Not Be Afraid to Ask

As you already know, the worst thing that can happen when you ask is that you get a "no" as a response. If you approach each interaction with a giving attitude and build a relationship first, you will be in a stronger position before you ask for help. Find a connection first, even if it is something as simple as the fact that you both grew up in the same state. Also, when you ask for something, make it easy for the person to say yes. For example, if you have a mentor, do not ask her to get you promoted in six months, but do ask her to coach you on how you can develop the skills that will make you more likely to be promoted by the various managers in the company.

Key 5 - Be a "Thought Leader"

You want to have something intriguing to say at all these lunches, dinners, and networking receptions. Strive to be a "thought leader," especially in your particular field. When you have something interesting to say, people will remember you when you follow up with them later. Also, once you are recognized as a thought leader, you should get yourself placed as a speaker or panel discussion participant at conferences and workshops. This is free PR to build your individual "brand" and enhance your scope of influence in your field. Also, it is amazingly easy to network when people are approaching *you* after your speech.

Key 6 - Volunteer

With a sincere, giving mindset, get involved – especially locally – in a way that is congruent with your strategic plan. Eventually, you want to get on the board of the organization where you volunteer. For example, I have a real passion for reaching back to help inner-city youth. Thus, I have worked for about eight years as a volunteer in Houston, Dallas, and Atlanta in the Leaders of Tomorrow (LOT) teen mentoring program. The LOT program is sponsored by the National Black MBA Association (NBMBAA). Eventually, I became a board member of NBMBAA-Atlanta, which allowed me to meet an eventual business partner for an online business. Of course, I did not know I would meet an eventual business partner in Atlanta when I started volunteering for LOT years before in Houston. However, it did make strategic sense for me to do my volunteering work under the umbrella of a professional organization of high-flyers (NBMBAA) rather than through another community organization.

Key 7 - Have a Reason to Follow Up

When you meet a high-flyer that can enhance your strategic plan, do not leave the conversation without a reason to follow up. Usually, this reason should be based on something you can volunteer to do to help them. For example, if you are a young med student and you meet your U.S. congressman at a reception, ask for his card so that you can volunteer for the next campaign. Tell the congressman about your friend who edits a video blog that might want to do an interview about the congressman's education bill. Remember, the goal of your networking efforts should not be an immediate gain for yourself. Ten years later, that same congressman may be in a position to help you get on an important public policy committee as you pursue your goal of being Surgeon General (see previous example). Before you follow up, ask the person how they want you to follow up (e.g., some people prefer a phone call on Friday morning, and some prefer e-mail).

Life Lesson:

When you meet a high-flyer that can enhance your strategic plan, do not leave the conversation without a reason to follow up.

Key 8 - Follow Up

Always follow up. The high-flyers that you want in your sphere of influence meet many people every day. Some follow up, but most do not. And when you do follow up, remember to be courteous to the person that answers the phone. It may be a secretary whose intention is to screen all calls. Be ready to give a compelling reason why the high-flyer should return your call. For example, the reason, "The congressman asked me to give him a call to help facilitate an interview with an influential blogger who happens to be a friend of mine. The interview may result in coverage of the congressman's reelection bid", is a compelling rationale to get the assistant to put your call through.

In summary, do not forget that networking can take place anywhere, at any time. So, be prepared and make sure you bring something to the table. Bring a business card, too, though you definitely want to get *their* contact information, whether they are carrying a business card or not. Like any other important activity, you must practice. Always be genuine; be yourself. Remember, networking not only enhances your survival; it also leads to your success.

> "The richest people in the world look for and build networks; everyone else looks for work. Marinate on that for a minute."
>
> — Robert Kiyosaki, entrepreneur
> and author of *Rich Dad, Poor Dad*

#DoItNow – What Actions Will You Take as a Result of Reading This Chapter?

1)

2)

3)

CHAPTER TEN

THE HERO'S JOURNEY

"There is what I would call the hero journey, the night sea journey, the hero quest, where the individual is going to bring forth in his life something that was never beheld before."

– Joseph Campbell, professor and author
of *The Hero with a Thousand Faces*

The Hero's Journey can provide an opening to find and empower your genuine self. Through completing your grand journey into the unknown, you can be of genuine service to others – and ultimately yourself.

What is the Hero's Journey? It is the familiar model of stories that involves a hero who goes on a quest, is triumphant and avoids calamity, and comes home different, improved, and victorious.

Life Lesson:

What is the Hero's Journey? It is the familiar model of stories that involves a hero who goes on a quest, is triumphant and avoids calamity, and comes home victorious.

"A hero is someone who has given his or her life to something bigger than oneself," according to acclaimed academic and author, Joseph Campbell. That means anyone can be a hero, by design or even by chance, but it requires a harrowing journey that is a precondition for eventual success. Fortunately, if your service-driven purpose is bigger than yourself, you will find the necessary courage already accessible to help you.

Both men and women are invited to answer the call of the herald, so you can be a "hero" or a "shero".

As summarized by Campbell, the Hero's Journey is basically:

> After encountering a 'herald' who calls the hero or heroine to something better… "A hero ventures forth from the world of common day into a region of supernatural wonder: fabulous forces are there encountered, and a decisive victory is won: the hero comes back from this mysterious adventure with the power to bestow [gifts] on his fellow man."

You want examples of The Hero's Journey? How about Beowulf, Odysseus in *The Odyssey*, the paraplegic Marine Jake Sully in *Avatar*, Simba in *The Lion King*, and Neo in *The Matrix*. From the Bible, there is Noah, Moses, and Joshua, to name a few.

Let's use Luke Skywalker in *Star Wars: Episode IV - A New Hope* as a specific example to shed light on The Hero's Journey. Look for parallels that you have personally faced *or will likely face* in the contexts of business, leadership, extended family, and your personal life. Then think of The Hero's Journey as a roadmap for you to reach your own primary goal – that thing that you crave with a burning desire.

First Stage – The Ordinary World

We meet our hero or heroine in their ordinary, mundane environment. The epic journey has yet to start, and we get to know details about the hero or heroine, their skills, and their attitude toward life.

Luke Skywalker does not have much. He is an unremarkable young man living on a farm with his aunt and uncle on a desolate desert planet called Tatooine.

Ask yourself, is there some part of your life in which you are stuck in the ordinary and mundane? Is there a part of your life you would like to transform?

> **Life Lesson:**
> Ask yourself, is there some part of your life in which you are stuck in the ordinary and mundane? Is there a part of your life you would like to transform?

Second Stage – The Call to Adventure

This is where our hero receives a call to action from a herald. An example of the call to adventure can be something that threatens him or his family or a disruption of the hero's ordinary world.

Through the droid R2-D2, Luke stumbles upon a message from Princess Leia asking for help from Obi-Wan Kenobi. This message immediately disturbs the comfort of Luke's ordinary world and presents an ordeal or test that must be commenced.

Or, as Joseph Campbell writes, "The hero's journey always begins with the call. One way or another, a guide must come to say, 'Look, you're in Sleepy Land. Wake. Come on a trip. There is a whole aspect of your consciousness, your being, that's not been touched. So, you're at home here? Well, there's not enough of you there. And so it starts."

Ask yourself, when it comes to transforming your life in the areas that are most important to you, is opportunity knocking? Are you answering the call?

Third Stage – Refusal of the Call

Here, the hero has deep personal doubts about the journey because he is afraid or not yet ready to leave the comfort of home.

Luke is not ready to leave his aunt, uncle, and his ordinary farm life on Tatooine, so he refuses the call.

Is fear holding you back? Chapter Four of this book talks about how you can *expand* your comfort zone by flipping the script as it relates to fear.

Fourth Stage – Meeting the Mentor / Helper

At this stage, the hero receives guidance from a mentor, which might include wise counsel, pragmatic coaching, or self-confidence. This mentoring dispels the hero's fears.

Luke is guided in the right direction by Obi-Wan Kenobi (known to Luke at this point as Ben Kenobi). This gives Luke the strength and daring to begin his Hero's Journey.

Are you coachable? What do you do when you receive wise counsel?

Fifth Stage – Crossing the Threshold

Now, the hero is ready to begin his quest. He may start eagerly, or he may be pushed, but either way, he crosses the threshold away from his familiar, ordinary world.

Luke returns to find the farm burned down and his aunt and uncle dead, killed by stormtroopers from the evil Empire. He is, of course, shocked and distraught about the murders. Now, he seems to wish he had answered the call sooner. Having no reason to stay on Tatooine, Luke decides to go with Ben Kenobi to learn to become a Jedi Knight and help deliver plans for the Death Star to the Rebel Alliance.

In your life or business, once you know what to do, do you take action?

Life Lesson:

Ask yourself, in your life or business, once you know what to do, do you take action?

Sixth Stage – Tests / Allies / Enemies

When the hero enters the new Special World, we notice a definite shift. The hero might be confused by this unfamiliar existence and its new rules. Now, out of his comfort zone, the hero is confronted with an ever more complicated series of challenges that test him in a variety of ways. He will meet allies and enemies. And, sometimes, friends turn out to be foes.

Luke's allies for this journey are Han Solo and Chewbacca, who agree to take Luke and Ben Kenobi to a planet called Alderaan.

Who are your allies? Undoubtedly, you have friends and family who, consciously or not, work for *You, Inc.* – a concept that is detailed in Chapter Twelve. What people or skillsets are currently *missing* from your virtual team?

Seventh Stage – Approach to the Innermost Cave

The innermost cave may represent a real location where lies a horrific danger or an inner struggle the Hero has not yet faced. At the threshold to the cave, doubts and fears can resurface for the hero. He must find the courage to continue.

By the time Luke and his allies arrived at Alderaan, the planet had been destroyed. They then manage to invade the evil Empire's Death Star and rescue Princess Leia.

When the going gets tough in your life or business career, how do you react?

Eighth Stage – Ordeal

This is where our hero hits rock bottom. Campbell describes it as the "belly of the whale", indicating some bleak news for the hero. The hero must now confront his greatest fear or most deadly foe. Only through some form of 'death' can the hero be born-again, experiencing a figurative resurrection that, in some way, endows him with greater strength or understanding.

The villain of *Star Wars*, Darth Vader, kills Luke's mentor, Ben Kenobi, with a lightsaber while Luke watches in horror. Luke manages to escape on Han Solo's spacecraft.

Think about a specific time when you hit rock bottom, personally or professionally. What did you do? What did you learn?

> **Life Lesson:**
>
> Ask yourself, when the going gets tough in your life or career, how do you react?

Ninth Stage – Reward

Our hero can see the light at the end of the tunnel. It is a point where the hero gains something after surviving death or mastering a special challenge. The reward may come in many forms: an object of great significance, a secret revealed, greater understanding, or even reconciliation with an ally.

In Luke's journey at this stage, he is transformed, as he finds the self-confidence to join the rebel forces that plan to take down Darth Vader's evil Empire. There is no time to celebrate; instead, Luke must now get ready for the final stages of his journey.

We reap what we sow. Ask yourself, what are you sowing to enable your reward?

Tenth Stage – The Road Back

Actually, the light at the end of the tunnel may be further away than the hero thought. At this stage, the hero is relieved and can go home.

He must choose between his own personal objective and another that is a higher calling.

Luke did have an opportunity to go home with Han Solo – a reverse to the original Call to Adventure – but Luke refused the opportunity. Luke, instead, stays and fights with the rebels against the Empire.

Sometimes, we must put a higher calling above our own short-term interests. In life and in business, if you assist enough folks as they strive for their dreams, your own dreams will come true.

Eleventh Stage – Atonement / Resurrection

This is the culmination of the story in which the hero must have his ultimate and most dangerous clash with death. The climactic battle also signifies something much larger than the hero's survival. The outcome will have a significant impact on his Ordinary World. Ultimately, the hero succeeds, wipes out his enemy, and comes out from battle purified and born-again, at least figuratively.

It is up to Luke to lead the rebels. With assistance from allies, Han Solo and Chewbacca, Luke defeats Darth Vader and obliterates the Death Star.

To reach your primary goal, what is the biggest challenge that you will have to overcome? Are you ready to do it now?

Twelfth Stage – Return with the Elixir

This is the triumphant homecoming when the hero returns to his Ordinary World as a transformed person. He successfully returns with the 'Elixir,' or the trophy won during his journey – either a physical prize or insights earned. His return may bring new hope to the Ordinary World or even a specific solution to their troubles.

In this final stage, our hero, Luke Skywalker, and the Rebels celebrate the destruction of the Death Star. Luke is given a medal and accolades for his courage.

If you reach your primary goal, how will that impact the people you care about the most?

Once the hero has returned to the so-called Ordinary World, after completing the 12 stages, things will never be the same again. We already learned from Campbell that a hero is someone who has given his or her life to something bigger than oneself. In the context of business and leadership, we often see the one who works the hardest (figuratively gives his or her life) rise to the top of an organization.

The concept works for families, as well. A parent may go on a Hero's Journey, sacrificing themselves so their children can have a better life. An example may be a working single mom who goes back to college part-time in the evenings so that she can one day graduate and elevate her career. Her motivation might be moving to a better neighborhood so the children can go to better schools and have other socioeconomic advantages.

And we repeatedly see – think Martin Luther King, Jr., Nelson Mandela, Mother Teresa, and Abraham Lincoln – that leaders add the most value to people when making sacrifices and serving others.

> **Life Lesson:**
>
> Leaders add the most value to people when making sacrifices and serving others.

When Campbell writes, *"The cave you fear to enter holds the treasure you seek,"* we can sense how this relates to running a business or leading a team. Who is the competitor that you must challenge head-on in the marketplace? What is the skill you have struggled to add, but you know is needed for you to be a better leader for your team?

Let's look at another business example. Presume that someone named Julie is an entrepreneur with an amazing idea that can disrupt an industry. She would love to have Shannon and her talents on the team as a partner, given Shannon's specific technology experience.

Julie can be the 'herald', inviting her good friend, Shannon, to address something that *Shannon* deeply cares about. Julie wants to help Shannon find a solution to her problems.

It could be that Shannon wants her children to not only graduate from college but to walk across the stage at graduation 100% debt-free. Shannon might want extra income so her spouse can stay at home with the kids instead of warehousing them in daycare. It could be that Shannon and her significant other want to retire 15 years early and have true time and financial freedom. Along the way, Shannon wants recognition in the industry for doing something amazing in the technology space.

When our new hero, Shannon, enters the new Special World of being a business co-owner, we notice a definite shift. Shannon might be confused by this unfamiliar existence and its new rules. Now, out of her comfort zone, Shannon is confronted with an ever more difficult series of challenges and competitors that test her in a variety of ways.

But Julie is there as a mentor to help the new business partner. With focused effort, our new hero, Shannon, can eventually enjoy the same amazing victory as the heroes that Campbell describes. And they can all return to their tribes as a hero, bearing gifts (e.g., extra income or time freedom).

"We must let go of the life we have planned, so as to accept the one that is waiting for us," according to Campbell. If you want to answer the call, just do it now!

"Being is not passive; it takes focused awareness."

— Maureen Murdock, author
of *The Heroine's Journey*

#DoItNow – What Actions Will You Take as a Result of Reading This Chapter?
1)
2)
3)

CHAPTER ELEVEN

A WEALTH OF FAMILY

"You don't choose your family. They are God's gift to you, as you are to them."

— Bishop Desmond Tutu, Nobel Peace Prize
Laureate and human rights activist

The family is a work of genius from nature, the most vital social unit of our civilization. It is primarily the family that ensures the continuation of humankind through procreation. The family sustains our culture through its role in the socialization of children. Mothers, fathers, and the immediate family form a child's first relationships.

A central theme of my adult life has been to find and sustain a balance between working hard, playing hard, workouts, and family relationships. When I am in balance, I am happy. However, sometimes we must work according to deadlines, and our career can take the lion's share of our time over an extended period. When that happens, our workouts and physical health can suffer. And quality time with those most important to you may be diminished. When we get out of life balance, we should aggressively seek to get back in balance at the earliest possible opportunity.

Life Lesson:

When we get out of life balance, we should aggressively seek to get back in balance at the earliest possible opportunity.

Love and support your immediate and extended family. I try to do that – though I am not perfect – and I also learned to realize I could not treat everyone equally. However, I do try to treat everyone fairly. Relationships are a two-way street and require two people exerting effort for them to grow.

I have learned from my mistakes when dealing with family, and the excellent books by Deepak Chopra have helped also. Now, I try to always bring a gift of some type, even if it is a compliment, blessing, or prayer. I now strive to make sure my actions are motivated by love, allowing me to do less and achieve more. This helps me resist defending my actions or my point of view and leaves me more open to hearing the views of others.

Life Lesson:

I strive to make sure my actions are motivated by love, allowing me to do less and achieve more. This helps me resist defending my actions or my point of view.

Growing up with my mother, Joan, we rarely had money to spare. As a single mother, she had her share of struggles. However, what we lacked in money, Joan more than compensated for with love.

Because of Joan's love and the many sacrifices she made to ensure I had, at least, a minimal amount of clothes and food, I see her as my real mother, just as if she had given birth to me herself. Though we had limited financial resources, she always put my needs above her own. She also maintained a well-kept home. Although I later came to know my biological mother, no one can take Joan's place, as she dedicated herself to giving me a strong foundation in life.

My childhood was not easy. As a young African American male, I battled racial stereotypes at school, even as I searched for a place among my peers. And amid life's normal chaos, Joan suddenly revealed to me in Spring 1978 – when I was 11 years old – that she was actually not my biological mother but that she had adopted me just months after my birth in 1966.

This shocking news rocked my world. At the time, I felt as though I had been living a lie for 11 years. I felt like there was no one I could talk to about my situation. All my cousins, except for one, did not even know that I had been adopted. I did not feel any of my friends would be understanding or supportive. I was in many ways alone. The reality of suddenly finding out that I was adopted left me hurt, confused, and resentful. I could not even sleep.

My caring mother tried to talk to me during the subsequent days, but I kept my feelings to myself. After about three weeks of quiet reflection, I began to accept that my adopted family completely loved me and cared about me. Because of this love, I decided that they were my *real* family. Apart from two brief discussions, I did not talk again to Joan about the adoption until 1992. To me, while in high school and college, there was really nothing to discuss. Joan loved me. She was my real mother. Her extended family – the Lowry family – was my real family. There was nothing more to say.

In my first book, *A Wealth of Family: An Adopted Son's International Quest for Heritage, Reunion, and Enrichment*, I wrote about my life with Joan, growing up as an African American boy on the north side of Pittsburgh. Joan provided a loving home and a devoted extended family. Even the shocking revelation by my mother that I had been adopted did not prevent me from following my ambitions to go to college and figuratively leave the ghetto behind.

Eventually, after doing my undergraduate studies in Pittsburgh, working in Texas, and then going to MBA school at the University of Maryland, I decided in 1992 – at the age of 25 – to search for my biological parents and fill in the missing gaps of my heritage.

Even though I had known of my adoption since I was eleven years old and had a particularly good relationship with my adoptive family, I felt a growing need to know more about my biological background. Because I knew nothing of my biological parents and their heritage, I felt somehow that my own human identity was partially lacking. I compare this sentiment with that of many African Americans whose family heritages were erased by centuries of slavery. However, in my case, even basic info about my biological parents was a mystery also.

"I was shocked to receive any information at all," I told my friends in 1992 after requesting – and getting – a letter summarizing my case from the agency that handled my adoption back in 1966. It was incredibly fulfilling to add pieces to the puzzle of my own identity. Though there were no names, addresses, or specific details in that initial letter, I learned that my biological mother was a white American who had descended from Lithuanian Jews. She gave birth to me at the age of nineteen. My biological father's family was from Kenya. I still considered myself to be an African American that had grown up in Pittsburgh – but I was now multi-ethnic, as well. Both of my biological parents had attended college. This was much more information than I had ever expected to receive, and it gave me a good feeling about the contribution of both biological families to my heritage.

I eventually searched for and found my white biological mother. I found her living in London, with my previously unknown British siblings. Subsequently, I also located my African biological family during my first trip to Nairobi. When I started my mission, I had no idea the search for my biological parents would take me around the world. My birth parents and their families were leading remarkable lives overseas.

My international quest to locate my biological parents and the resulting reunions have profoundly affected me and three radically different families in the United States, Great Britain, and Kenya. It is a story that I hope will inspire people to explore their own lives, cultures, and relationships.

What I learned was anything but ordinary. I have discovered that there is a great deal in my heritage of which to be proud. There are the courage and integrity of my Kenyan family and the challenges they have overcome. My ancestors' odyssey on my biological mother's side, who escaped the murderous persecution of the Orthodox Russians against Lithuanian Jews, is impressive and compelling. There is my individual piece in the large and grand African American experience, growing up in a dynamic family in Pittsburgh.

I have been told that my true story of adoption, reunion, and heritage provides a timely and inspiring perspective on multicultural families and provocative prescriptions to address racism and poverty.

I love the opportunities I now get to inspire people with my multicultural adoption story. I have been fortunate to speak to companies, small businesses, professional organizations, conference attendees, universities, adoption & foster care agencies, religious groups, and even at high school commencements. I am told that my story resonates well with anyone who cares about the concept of family.

"I sustain myself with the love of family."

— Maya Angelou, poet, author, and civil rights activist

#DoItNow – What Actions Will You Take as a Result of Reading This Chapter?
1)
2)
3)

CHAPTER TWELVE

SHOW ME YOUR FRIENDS, AND I'LL SHOW YOU YOUR FUTURE

"No person is your friend who demands your silence, or denies your right to grow."

— Alice Walker, Pulitzer Prize-winning novelist

You are the average of the five people you spend the most time with. That well-known saying was attributed most often to legendary motivational speaker Jim Rohn. The implication is that you will want to choose your friends and associates very carefully. They will influence or enhance or sabotage the paths you take. Develop friends with diverse backgrounds and talents who positively challenge you in all areas. The primary handicap a person has is typically the people around them.

Life Lesson:

Friends will enhance or sabotage the paths you take. Develop friends with diverse backgrounds who positively challenge you in all areas.

It has been said, "show me your friends, and I'll show you your future." This basic concept has been around since, at least, the days of the Old Testament (Proverbs 13:20). Do not only make friends who are comfortable to be with. Make friends who will challenge you to be a better and more successful person. As you and your friends grow individually, you do not have to grow apart.

A case in point is that I joined some of my Alpha Phi Alpha fraternity brothers who started taking regular vacation trips in the mid-1990s that we referred to as the ABT, or 'All Boyz Trip'. We live in different parts of the country. Since all of us grew up in urban environments, we make certain these trips allow us to get in touch with nature. We visited the Grand Canyon, California Wine Country, and Yosemite National Park. White water rafting in Montana's Glacier National Park was outstanding but brutally cold. We then used our brains to plan the subsequent trip and went sailing in the warm British Virgin Islands. The ABT has frequented Cancun and the nearby Mayan ruins. We skied in Breckenridge and Park City. While surrounded by nature, we discuss how we can be better people, better husbands to our wives, and better men in general. We taught each other a lot about friendship. We share the problems we have with our extended families. We do not let each other down when it really matters and continually encourage each other to dream about different dimensions of success. We always share our goals with each other and provide constructive criticism when our fellow brother is screwing up. Thanks to my friends, as well as my own character and determination, I survived some tough periods, and I always found a way to advance through them. Anyone can benefit from a group of friends like these guys.

"Friends are the family you choose," according to peace activist, Edna Buchman. Do not spend time with people – friends, family, or significant others – who disparage your aspirations and dreams. Make sure your friends will push you, motivate you, and inspire you.

Life Lesson:

Do not spend time with people who disparage your aspirations and dreams. Make sure your friends will push you, motivate you, and inspire you.

Beyond the fun and brotherhood of my close friendships, I also view my friends as a 'virtual board of directors' to advise me. I got this concept from a superb article in *Fortune* magazine way back in January 1996.

The article's concept is that even if you work in corporate America – regardless of the company name on your paycheck – you are already in business *for yourself* today. What your paycheck should say is "You, Inc." since you are effectively self-employed for all practical purposes. You are responsible for your own career and long-term wealth generation.

Here's how it works, according to the article. You are the chief executive officer of a little company whose mission is to persuade people to buy your services. Undoubtedly, you have friends and family who, consciously or not, work for You, Inc. The significance of this exercise is to help you see who they are, what they do, and whether they do it well – and most importantly – whether there are crucial individuals missing from your virtual organization.

Up or out. Grow or die. These concepts apply to individuals as well as businesses. Build your own personal board of directors accordingly.

You, Inc. might not ever hold a staff meeting. It may only exist in a corner of your mind. However, it still needs stellar staff. A good CEO must be able to attract and retain top talent. You want people on your team that know more than you when it comes to their functional area.

CEO: You are the chief executive officer, and no one but you can provide the vision, principles, and leadership for You, Inc. Make sure that your board and staff fully endorse your vision and standards and comprehend how they can advance the strategies and tactics of You, Inc.

Finance Department: You will probably act as your own chief financial officer. Your tax department (CPA), treasurer (stockbroker), and banker effectively report directly to you. If the job gets to be so onerous that you are earning good money but not managing it well, bring in a professional financial planner.

General Counsel: Most people I know have a friend who is a lawyer that they can talk to informally. If you do not have such a person, then network through your friends. That lawyer friend or acquaintance will be able to refer you to other lawyers if your issues are not in their wheelhouse. Being referred by your lawyer friend is often better than finding specific law expertise through a Google search.

Chief Operating Officer: If you are in corporate America, this is your boss. Flip the script. She actually works for you, at least in the context of You, Inc. Her job is managing your day-to-day operations, making sure things move forward efficiently. She is *not* typically responsible for your long-range planning or decisions to enter new markets – such as working for other companies or becoming an entrepreneur. By the way, your boss only works for you conceptually. She may think she is in charge. Maintain harmony and let her keep thinking that.

By the way, if your boss virtually works for you, then that means you work for your subordinates. Make sure you are helping them reach their strategic objectives. Sometimes, a subordinate who eventually passes you up in the organization can be the best thing to happen in your career, if you treated them well.

Chief Technology Officer: Technology is vast and moves fast. I recommend that you have multiple virtual CTOs to give you the expertise you need in diverse technology areas. Always look for new people with new capabilities that you can add to the team. Remember that You, Inc. is in perpetual competition with *THEM, LLC* in America, in addition to *THEIR, Co., Ltd* in Japan and *THEY, GmbH* in Germany. Being knowledgeable about information technology can make all of the difference for your success in the global marketplace.

Marketing VP: Elite athletes and actors have them – they are known as agents – and you should have one also. These people make it a point to push opportunities in your direction. The Marketing VP might be an executive in your company, a mentor who publicizes your talents, or a headhunter who wants to enable the next phase of your career. A former boss or a satisfied customer can do the trick, as well. And if you want a good Marketing VP, then be one for others. Start advocating for someone you respect.

Joining you, the chairman, should be these inside board members: your spouse or significant other, and maybe a parent or mature child.

Your board of directors for You, Inc. is responsible for giving it to you straight as they offer their guidance. Board members not only receive no compensation, but they may not even know they are part of You, Inc. I am quite fortunate. My close friends have been great outside board members because they provide me with candor, without sugarcoating, which is just how I like it. If you want empathy, get the appropriate person on your board who can meet you where you are.

If you can show me your friends, then I will show you your future.

Your board of directors can even include an imaginary member who is called in when the CEO needs confidential counseling. This is similar to the "Invisible Counselors" in Napoleon Hill's *Think and Grow Rich*. Your imaginary counselors can be everyone from Abraham Lincoln to Barack Obama. From Bob Dylan to The Notorious B.I.G. Or, from Andrew Carnegie to Oprah Winfrey.

Speaking of Oprah, she once explained, *"Lots of people want to ride with you in the limo, but what you want is someone who will take the bus with you when the limo breaks down."* Sometimes, it is not that we must rely on our friends for tangible help, but the fact that we know they are there for us sustains our confidence as we face difficult times.

Will your friends stick with you when times are tough? Make sure they will if you have them on the board of You, Inc.

Life Lesson:

Will your friends stick with you when times are tough? Make sure they would if you have them in your inner circle.

Just as the best time to raise an army is well before the war starts, you will want to develop and invest in your close friendships long before you need them.

"If friends disappoint you over and over, that's in large part your own fault. Once someone has shown a tendency to be self-centered, you need to recognize that and take care of yourself; people aren't going to change simply because you want them to."

— Oprah Winfrey, billionaire host, TV producer, actress, author, and philanthropist

#DoItNow – What Actions Will You Take as a Result of Reading This Chapter?

1)

2)

3)

CHAPTER THIRTEEN

SEX, LOVE, AND OTHER DRUGS

"Sex, drugs, and rock 'n' roll. Take out the drugs and you've got more time for the other two."

— **Steven Tyler, Aerosmith lead singer and television personality**

We know their names: Whitney Houston, Len Bias, Jimi Hendrix, Prince, Heath Ledger, DMX, and Michael Jackson.

These iconic celebrities are reported to have all died of causes related to acute drug use. Some were using legal prescription drugs, and others were using illegal drugs. According to the National Center of Health Statistics, more than 67,000 Americans died from a drug-involved overdose in 2018 alone. Fatal overdoses are highly associated with drugs such as opiates, cocaine, and alcohol.

This can happen to young people, too. Baseball pitcher, Tyler Skaggs, died in 2019 at the young age of 27. He apparently choked on his own vomit while under the influence of alcohol, fentanyl, and oxycodone. He was found dead in his hotel room.

Another baseball player, José Fernández, died in 2016 at the age of 24, when he crashed his 32-foot boat in a pre-dawn accident off the coast of Miami. The two passengers on the boat with him were also killed. From the autopsy and toxicology reports released a month later, we know Fernandez was legally drunk and had cocaine in his system.

Actor and musician, River Phoenix, died of a drug overdose in Los Angeles in October 1993 at age 23. The official cause of his death was acute multiple drug intoxication, including cocaine and morphine.

Teens can be impacted, as well. Actress Anissa Jones from the old sitcom, "A Family Affair", died at the age of 18 after a party. The cause was an accidental drug overdose. She had cocaine, PCP, and other drugs in her system.

It may be that celebrities are taking drugs partly due to the additional pressure of being at the top of their profession. It may be that they are missing the work/life balance that so many of us strive to maintain. However, deaths from drug use happen to people who are not famous also.

I am not going to write a chapter on alcohol and drug addiction. Plenty of books have been produced to cover substance abuse and addiction in well-researched detail. However, be aware that addiction is possible with prescription drugs, including sleeping pills, anti-depressants, and pain killers – in addition to illegal drugs obtained from local dealers. You can even become addicted to the caffeine found in coffee and other common drinks. Caffeine may have side effects such as sleep disruption, anxiety, and depression. Anyone who starts using tobacco can become addicted to nicotine, and that has serious health implications, including death.

While I am not going to write extensively on drug addiction, I will remind you to stay on the right side of the law. Be disciplined when it comes to keeping your record clean. Do not break any laws: local, state, federal, or foreign. You do not want to shipwreck your future. Having *any* type of criminal record can potentially negatively impact your future – whether it is a future job in corporate America, a medical license, a law license, or a small business loan. Stay out of the criminal justice system. Note that I am not just talking about the law against underage drinking – another huge concern is the *additional laws* often broken by teens and young adults when they drink alcohol. Avoid any potentially negative encounters with law enforcement officers.

Life Lesson:

Stay on the right side of the law. Be disciplined when it comes to keeping your record clean. Do not break any laws. You do not want to shipwreck your future.

Since 1984, the minimum legal drinking age everywhere in the United States was 21 years. According to the U.S. Centers for Disease Control and Prevention, drinking by those below the age of 21 is strongly linked with the following issues:

- Death from alcohol poisoning
- Unintentional injuries, such as car crashes, falls, burns, and drowning
- Suicide and violence, such as fighting and sexual assault
- Changes in brain development
- School performance problems, such as higher absenteeism and poor or failing grades

- Alcohol dependence later in life
- Other *dangerous behaviors,* such as smoking, drug misuse, and risky sexual behaviors

Yes, alcohol is legal if you are of a certain age, but alcohol is still a drug. Marijuana is already legal in 11 states as of late 2020, but it is still a drug. And I would argue that the above-bulleted list of consequences is still disproportionally impacting young adults through, at least, age 26. Be careful.

To be safe, avoid risky situations. If you want to stay sober and avoid alcohol and drugs, do not socialize with people that you know use drugs and do not hang out where you used to drink.

Life Lesson:

To be safe, avoid risky situations. If you want to stay sober and avoid alcohol and drugs, do not socialize near or with people that you know use these substances.

Of course, you do not have to rush into sexual activity. That applies to you at any age, and it applies to any new relationship. If you choose to have sex, mixing alcohol or drugs with sex often leads to STDs and unplanned pregnancies when safe sex practices are overlooked due to impaired judgment.

You want to make good decisions. Sometimes, that means learning from the mistakes of others. NFL quarterback, Jameis Winston, unfortunately, has a track record of alleged bad decisions. It was reported (bit.ly/3mamLQZ) that he caused thousands of dollars in damages in an apartment complex near Florida State University due to an incident with a BB gun in 2012. He was also accused (bit.ly/2RdJ5ef) of shoplifting crab legs in a separate incident in Tallahassee.

More seriously, Winston was accused in 2012 of sexual assault while in college – he was eventually cleared of criminal charges in 2014 (bit.ly/32h21PH). The woman ultimately filed a civil suit against Winston, and they reached a settlement agreement in 2016 (bit.ly/32jn83R). Winston claimed that the encounter was consensual.

If that was not enough, Winston was accused of groping a female Uber driver in 2016. After an investigation, based on the incident and his bad track record, the NFL suspended him for 3 games at the start of the 2018 season (bit.ly/3mbrB0r). Winston publicly apologized to the Uber driver and claimed he had "eliminated alcohol" from his life. Hopefully, Winston has finally learned his lesson and will stay sober and make better decisions.

How can we avoid the drama related to drugs and put the spotlight on the pursuit of our dreams?

We can leverage the power of our subconscious minds to select preferences related to what we correlate with discomfort. We can select similar preferences related to what we correlate with enjoyment. We can link *both* positive and negative feelings to anything. It is our choice. Think of food (feasting vs. fasting can both be good) as one example where we can apply this idea. Think of sex (loving sex vs. abstinence can both be good) as another good example.

Here is an additional perspective. Strenuous daily workouts at the gym can be good or bad (long-term health vs. overuse injuries, or even using workouts to avoid problems with your significant other).

And finally, prescription opioids can be helpful or risky (opioid treatment for pain vs. non-drug pain management techniques for safety, such as massage and acupuncture). It is about consequences and specifically using your mind to avoid the negative consequences that result from the various forms of addiction.

Humans like to avoid discomfort. We would rather repeat tasks that give us joy.

Sometimes, we duck and dodge from the "main thing" that would improve the way we live, learn, work, and play because we have linked discomfort with doing the main thing.

Instead, we can turn that around. We can, as a substitute, correlate enjoyment with doing the main thing. For example, if we are in a sales role but are afraid of rejection, that can stop us from doing the main thing – calling on potential prospects. In this case, we need to draw a parallel with the task of making calls to the most fun thing we have ever done. Maybe when you make enough calls, you treat yourself and do that fun thing again. When we do this, we are then able to "keep the main thing the main thing," as Stephen Covey famously said. That will help yield money, financial freedom, and time freedom.

We can attribute any feeling to a thought that we want. For example, we can choose to be happy and excited about talking to potential sales prospects. We can figuratively think of our phone as a wealth creation machine when we use it to build our business.

We all face temptation. But why do we sometimes do things that are likely to hurt us, such as abusing drugs? Use your subconscious mind to help flip the script. Correlate using drugs with distressing things, such as job loss, damaged relationships, and health risks. Link not using drugs to positive, enjoyable things, such as success, wealth, family time, and love.

Life Lesson:

Correlate using drugs with distressing things, such as job loss, damaged relationships, and health risks. Link not using drugs to positive, enjoyable things such as success.

In life, we all make decisions. We must remember that we are responsible for the short and long-term consequences of those decisions.

"I don't need drugs. I want to be high on life with an overdose of you."

— Unknown

#DoItNow – What Actions Will You Take as a Result of Reading This Chapter?
1)
2)
3)

CHAPTER FOURTEEN

SAVE YOUR MARRIAGE
BEFORE IT STARTS

---

*"Love is like a baby. It needs
to be treated tenderly."*

— African Proverb

My first marriage was rocky from the beginning. My first spouse was a great person and a beautiful woman, but we were a bad match as a couple. I should have realized this during our engagement. We got married young – in our early twenties.

Marriage can be beautiful. However, in the 21st century, that usually happens when two people wait until they are 28 or 30 or older, giving them ample time to know themselves and each other.

If you are over the age of 30 now, think back to when you were 21 years old (and if you are currently well under 30, ask your parents or someone else older than you these questions). Do you like the same music that you did then? Are you practicing the same religion as you did then? Are you in the specific career that you planned when you were 21 years old? Are you now living in the city you planned to live in back when you were 21 years old? Have your expectations of your partner changed when it comes to sex? What physical characteristics do you now value to determine if someone is "good-looking"? Have your politics evolved since then? What is your view about having children and how you would like to raise them?

Most people need until they are in their late twenties (or early thirties) to settle into who they are really going to be.

Do not rush marriage. Part of not painting yourself into a corner is to prevent unplanned pregnancies with safe sex practices. And even if a baby is on the way, that does not necessarily mean that you should get married. A rocky marriage may not be in the best interest of the child.

Life Lesson:

Most people need until they are in their late twenties or early thirties to settle into who they are really going to be. Do not rush marriage.

As I described in my first book, *A Wealth of Family*, I learned a lot from my first marriage. And I learned even more in the relationships that followed before I met my fun and beautiful wife, Nikki. For most of us, complete happiness eventually includes some relationship with a significant other. Over the long haul, most of us need someone with whom to share career success, financial gains, fun activities, spirituality, family life, and fitness goals. It is also great to have a supportive partner to help you through any challenging times.

You do not necessarily need to find your "soul mate" right away to have this area of life in check. The goal is to just be comfortable with what you want for yourself, what you want in a significant other, and to be comfortable with how you are looking for your partner. The rest is just a matter of time. Once you get to this point, you can then free your mental energy to focus on other parts of your life, such as career, finances, health, and extended family, whether you are currently in a relationship or not.

When I decided that I was open to meeting a long-term prospective mate, I made the philosophical commitment to myself to not ask for things in the relationship that I was unable or unwilling to give. For example, I could not expect to get a highly disciplined mate in terms of her thinking, activities, and goal setting if I were unorganized, undisciplined, and severely lacking in these areas. What we get out of a relationship has a lot to do with what we give to our partner. The list of what you are asking for should be somewhat influenced by what we can give.

Life Lesson:

Make the philosophical commitment to yourself to not ask for things in a relationship that you are not willing and able to give.

American author, Aleatha Romig, is quoted as stating, "You don't marry someone you can live with; you marry the person who you cannot live without."

Here is a list of some qualities I considered in the women I dated. I prioritized my list with the "must-haves" at the top. Determining the ranking and the weight that each item carries is *your own personal decision.* This process of creating your list can take days or months. That is okay. However, I think each item is worth thinking about seriously, and I advise both men and women to start their own similar list.

For myself, I looked for someone who:

- Is honest and open
- Has "chemistry" with me, with mutual like growing to mutual love
- Has aesthetic good looks (a relatively shallow category)
- Is an exciting, compatible sexual partner
- Has no sexually transmitted diseases (only testing can verify this)
- Balances life—works hard, plays hard, and works out hard
- Hangs well with my friends and is a good friend to me
- Is happy in their career, ambitious with a shared life vision
- Is drug-free
- Keeps their word
- Is a good partner, advisor, and potential parent of children, as applicable
- Challenges and encourages me in all areas of life
- Has diverse, practical intelligence
- Is compatible in terms of problem-solving and handling disagreements
- Has financial status/future/discipline on par with me
- Has a sense of humor
- Accepts me for what and how I am
- Has diverse abilities, mindset, friends, activities, music, and other interests

- Is disciplined in thinking, activities, decisions, and goal setting
- Is confident, not possessive
- Has stable and healthy relationships with their own family and friends
- Is compatible spiritually in terms of beliefs, activities, and commitment
- Is astrologically compatible (a lower priority, but still fun for many)

Of course, each person's list of desired qualities for a relationship will vary. For most people, it will be shorter than mine. Think of the list shown here as a *memory jogger* for what is important for you.

Life Lesson:

Each person's list of desired qualities for a relationship will vary. Think of the list shown here as a memory jogger for what is important for you.

Once I had my ranked list in place, and I was willing and able to give everything on my list, my mind and spirit were free and open to meeting the right person. If I met someone, and after a while, I decided that they did not meet my prioritized needs, I then had a framework for how to deal with that person. For example, I could have kept her as a workout partner or a peer mentor for my professional career. Or I could have moved her out of my life completely. Whatever choice I made, I eventually learned to communicate my intentions clearly and consistently so that there were no misunderstandings. I expected the same respectful treatment in return from the woman. The framework allowed me to stay in control of my emotions and decisions.

My advice to friends on relationships and many other subjects is, "Don't passively avoid pain, proactively seek happiness and pleasure." When applied to relationships, this means to put yourself in a position to meet the type of people specified by your personal list. This does not mean acting desperately, just proactively. People can join professional organizations or do community service. Go to house parties where the guest list is somewhat filtered. Join a ski club, a scuba diving club, a travel club, or a running club. Actively pursue spiritual beliefs. Learn another language. In short, be yourself and live up to your own requirements list, and you will soon meet someone who also will live up to your list. The mindset and process described above prepared me to meet Nikki and enabled us to start our dating relationship on solid footing. After we met, we dated for about a year, spending a lot of time together. Then we got engaged, and she moved in with me during our engagement. We did pre-marriage counseling – not for any particular problem – but to improve our communication skills with each other. We have been happily married since 2001.

And when you find the right person, continue to create new possibilities together for the rest of your life. Put in the work to make it last. As Beyoncé sang, "I don't know much about fighting, but I know I will fight for you."

"To the extent that there's a lesson learned from another marriage, the thing that I tell lots of young couples is that marriage is hard work. Even the best of marriages require a lot of work."

— Michelle Obama, attorney, author and former
First Lady of the United States

#DoItNow – What Actions Will You Take as a Result of Reading This Chapter?

1)

2)

3)

CHAPTER FIFTEEN

FIRST IMPRESSIONS

"If you want to make a good first impression, smile at people. What does it cost to smile? Nothing. What does it cost not to smile? Everything, if not smiling prevents you from enchanting people."

— Guy Kawasaki, marketing specialist, author, and venture capitalist

Although first impressions may not be reliable, you probably know that you only get one chance to make that initial impression. This applies to social situations and to your career and/or entrepreneurial endeavors.

When I was in corporate America, I was not very conservative when it came to my attire in the workplace *once I was established* in my role. However, when you are making a first impression – especially in a job interview – you will likely want to err on the side of conformity if you want to improve your chances for success. This starts but does not end with professional attire.

Typically, people are judgmental. People make decisions without having all the information. They make these judgments from their "gut" based on "programs" running in their subconscious mind.

Life Lesson:

People typically make decisions without having all the information. They make these judgments based on "programs" running in their subconscious mind.

What are these automatic programs? Let us look at a few examples. When I say "Democrats," you have a certain way that you feel before hearing any other details. The same would be true when I say, "Republicans." What if I bring up New Yorkers, Texans, or people from Southern California? Or England or France or Russia or China? The mere mention of certain sports teams and rivalries – Steelers vs. Cowboys, Bears vs. Packers, Yankees vs. Red Sox, Tar Heels vs. Blue Devils, Penguins vs. Capitals – can generate a strong reaction based on the automatic programs for how you feel about each team.

There are social norms in the business world. And these social norms provide – fairly or unfairly – the automatic programs that will be used to judge you. People will take less than 15 seconds to form their first impression of you based on your attire, hairstyle, posture, handshake, and smile.

Now, some will say, "I should be able to dress or wear my hair any way I want to. That has nothing to do with my performance on the job." That may be true, but you probably want to maximize your chances of getting the job or winning the client if you are an entrepreneur. Know that you will get more latitude from bosses, colleagues, and customers after you are in the job or role and firmly established as a high performer.

Life Lesson:

You will get more latitude from bosses, colleagues, and customers after you are in the job or role and firmly established as a high performer.

You get just one opportunity to make a first impression, and a good reputation built over time can be ruined with one incident. Demonstrate appropriate speech, attire, and behavior in each situation. This applies both inside and outside of the workplace. And be on time when making that first impression.

Be aware that your interview (or sales call, if you are an entrepreneur) begins from the moment you arrive. You are being evaluated based on how you walk, how you look, and how you speak. This includes receptionist and administrative assistants – they are evaluating you, too.

The 12x12x12 rule from Dr. Ivan Misner, founder of BNI, the world's largest business networking organization, makes your networking or interviewing interactions more effective. For example, from 12 feet away, someone can observe your posture and attire. From 12 inches, grooming habits are noticeable, including bad breath, as well as eye contact. And the first 12 words you speak say a lot about you. Therefore, you want to have an introduction ready on the tip of your tongue. All these factors have an impact on your first impression.

What about the freedom to do what you want? Yes, freedom is a benefit of living in many western democracies, such as the United States. However, freedom and freedom from consequences are two vastly different things altogether.

Perception is often reality, rightly or wrongly.

Life Lesson:

Perception is often reality, rightly or wrongly.

The good news is that you can influence a person's perception of you. While you cannot please every boss, customer, and colleague, you can choose specific attributes of your personality that you like and make sure you put an emphasis on those attributes, especially when you meet new people. Be yourself, specifically your best self.

When it comes to business, I try to highlight a set of qualities that I call "F-5": Focused, fast, flexible, flawless, and fun. Being focused lets people know that I am serious. Being fast is important because success loves speed. I am flexible because you never know what humans will do, and the perceived needs of customers often change. While I am clearly *not* even close to flawless, I do project an air that is all about attention to detail. And finally, I am fun. What is more attractive – in business or in life – than someone who is earning money and having fun?

I am intentional when making a first impression to come across as genuinely focused, fast, flexible, flawless, and fun. It does not matter if I am in an interview, a client meeting, or just at a networking event. However, I am not suggesting that you use my "F-5". Find the positive attributes of *your own* personality that you want to highlight and then exude those qualities with enthusiasm and authenticity.

And make sure you smile!

"Two things remain irretrievable:
time and a first impression."

— Cynthia Ozick, writer, novelist, and essayist

#DoItNow – What Actions Will You Take as a Result of Reading This Chapter?
1)
2)
3)

CHAPTER SIXTEEN

BRING SOLUTIONS,
NOT JUST PROBLEMS

"The real problem is not the bad guys; it is that good guys have gone to sleep."

— Maynard Jackson, first African
American mayor of Atlanta

Be known for consistently bringing recommendations, solutions, and new possibilities to the table, not just problems.

Being recognized for reliably delivering solutions to the team enhances your personal brand. Of course, you must identify a problem first before a solution can be developed. You have to clearly understand the details of the problem to solve it. Do not cover up the problem.

Life Lesson:

Being recognized for reliably delivering solutions to the team enhances your personal brand.

Whatever we want to do and whatever problem we want to solve, everything that actually happens is a result of some *dialogue*. If it is a problem you are facing alone, you have a dialogue with yourself. For example, "What would I have to do? Am I good enough? What am I committed to?"

When you are assembling a team to solve a problem, it is about getting people, figuratively speaking, to be on the same side of the table. The team generates dialogue that leads to reflection and encourages people to agree on a common definition of the problem. Give people a safe space to brainstorm the problem definition and potential solutions. Inclusion is about respecting the differences – the actions and social norms that make certain that people feel welcome at the table. While you want the commitment of everyone on the team, note that they are "signing in" on the mission related to the problem that has to be solved and not necessarily the solution at this point in the journey. The initial dialogue should have a unifying purpose without pre-judging the solution.

You will eventually need a dialogue with other individuals to get them on board as allies. They must sign on voluntarily. Some people call this enrollment, which is a crucial team-building skill that can result in goal alignment and dedication across the team. Think about the many letters and conversations between Winston Churchill and Franklin D. Roosevelt to get the U.S. fully engaged as a World War II ally, to collaborate on shared priorities for major war initiatives, and ultimately, to prepare for post-war peace and rebuilding.

Let us look at a business example that takes advantage of enrollment dialogue. Imagine you work in marketing and are responsible for launching a product for your company. Your boss expects coherent product positioning as part of the marketing and public relations plan. You want to deliver a compelling solution to your boss. You have the product's technical specifications, but you are not entirely sure how those specifications will benefit the target customers. And how will these features benefit the end customer of your target customers?

The engineering team may not feel that they have some of those answers. However, you want them to sign on to the possibility of creating the right positioning so that you can successfully launch your product and win customers. So, you must master the invitation.

"Hey Joe, would it be OK if we schedule some time?

I would like to collaborate with you about [the problem].

I want to ensure a successful product launch.

I don't possess all the answers, but I am sure we can figure it out together.

So, Joe, when can we meet?"

After you are engaged in this dialogue with Joe and the engineering team, listen carefully to see how they react. People are often tuned in to a magical radio station called WIII-FM — which means, "What is in it for me?" Maybe the engineer that can help you the most is looking for the recognition associated with designing a product that ultimately has commercial success in the marketplace. Maybe he owns patents for the project and wants royalties if the product is successful. Or perhaps he is looking to advance his rank within the company or even outside.

Find the common ground. What may seem like a possibility to create a great solution in the eyes of your boss may be *perceived* by the engineering team as extra or unnecessary work. Your audience's perception matters a lot. Revealing the common ground that you have together can help to shift perceptions.

> **Life Lesson:**
> When you are assembling a team to solve a problem, it is about getting people, figuratively speaking, to be on the same side of the table. Find the common ground.

As another example, let us say Betty got a disappointing raise last year with her end-of-year performance review, in spite of the fact that her performance was graded as stellar. This can happen because, sometimes, 3% could be the highest raise granted by the company based on their business environment – regardless of the employee's individual performance.

Betty can simply use that disappointing event as a reminder to create the possibility of a solution – that her long-term priority is to build her own independent business. Yes, Betty is disappointed about the raise, but she does not have to endure feelings of suffering over it. Remember, we can connect any feeling to a thought that we want. After all, Betty may have already decided that by the end of next year, her monthly passive recurring income from her own part-time business will enable her to leave her day job. Now, the disappointing raise is a positive motivation for her long-term future.

Another example of crafting new possibilities is when you attach love to the idea of helping others – you now welcome obstacles, and you can overcome the obstacles relatively easily to create new solutions. For example, in my mentoring work with high school students, I am motivated by my love for helping the next generation of rising stars. With this motivation, solutions to problems – such as meeting space availability, having enough mentors, and funding for the program – seem to materialize more easily than you might expect.

At work or in your personal life, creating a new possibility or a solution often runs against conventional wisdom. Yes, you need to be aware of reality – but not limited by it. You can create a new future.

Life Lesson:

Creating a new possibility or a solution often runs against conventional wisdom. Yes, you need to be aware of reality – but not limited by it.

In the women's suffrage movement, there had to be dialogue. For decades, the movement did not reach their goals while correctly arguing the fact that "women and men are created equal". In the end, right or wrong, the politically more persuasive argument was that women should be able to vote because they were *different* than men – that their femininity and maternal leanings deserved a voice. To add to the dialogue, during World War I, women's work on behalf of the war effort proved they were just as patriotic and deserving as men. Today, we can see that this was a great decision. Women not only vote in huge numbers, but we also now have a number of great, *extremely qualified* women politicians up and down the ballot. One day soon, the U.S. may have its first woman president.

Dr. Nelson Mandela was a visionary. He fought for years in South Africa against apartheid, which is a system of complete racial segregation. He was arrested and imprisoned in 1962. Subsequently, in 1964, Mandela and six others were sentenced to life imprisonment and sent to notorious Robben Island to serve their sentences. In 1973, he was offered release if he would just go into exile. Instead, he chose to stay in prison for his cause. Mandela was not released until 1990 after a total of 27 years in prison. Along the way, he rallied South Africans – and most of the world – behind his cause. Once he was out of prison, Mandela led the negotiations to end apartheid. He was committed to creating a new solution for a new future. In 1994, a triumphant Mandela became South Africa's first black president.

Dr. Martin Luther King, Jr. was gifted in the ability to communicate and enroll people in the possibility of a brighter future. He made personal connections. He was willing to travel to any place where injustice and discrimination controlled daily life. Part of his dialogue with America included his extensive writings – he wrote five books and many articles. Dr. King led the Southern Christian Leadership Conference (SCLC), and he used his influence to coordinate efforts with other civil rights organizations, such as the Student Nonviolent Coordinating Committee and the National Association for the Advancement of Colored People. The SCLC coordinated voter registration drives all over the South. And the SCLC played a major role in the 1963 March on Washington. King's "*I Have a Dream*" speech is probably the greatest example of enrollment dialogue in our nation's history. He encouraged Americans to sign on to his wonderful dream, which still resonates with people today. Leaders drive dialogue about solutions while followers get stalled by problems.

Never lose hope. Peter Drucker stated, "The best way to predict the future is to create it." There's also a famous African proverb, "If you want to go fast, go alone. If you want to go far, go together." And the best way to bring new solutions to problems is to have the dialogue to get people – a collaborative team – to sign on to the idea of new potential possibilities. Just do it now!

> "You create opportunities by
> performing, not complaining."
>
> — Muriel Siebert, first female member
> of the New York Stock Exchange

#DoItNow – What Actions Will You Take as a Result of Reading This Chapter?
1)
2)
3)

CHAPTER SEVENTEEN

TWO EARS, ONE MOUTH

"We have two ears and one mouth so that we can listen twice as much as we speak."

— Epictetus, Greek Stoic philosopher

Most people do not listen to others with the objective of comprehension; instead, they partially listen as they plan their response to share their viewpoint. There is probably no better way to show someone that you admire and appreciate them than to genuinely listen to them. Here are some ideas to cultivate you as a great listener.

Look for and listen for the best in people. Albert Einstein once said, *"Everybody is a genius. But if you judge a fish by its ability to climb a tree, it will live its whole life believing that it is stupid."*

To discover the best in people, there are numerous strategies we can undertake to become better listeners.

Focus on being interested, not interesting. People absolutely love talking about themselves. If you are a ready listener, you will be extremely popular.

156

> **Life Lesson:**
>
> Focus on being interested, not interesting. People absolutely love talking about themselves. If you are a ready listener, you will be extremely popular.

And when you listen, make sure the other person knows you are engaged by asking sincere questions. "Knowledge speaks, but wisdom listens," is a quote attributed to the legendary musician, Jimi Hendrix.

Find common ground. This is especially important during a negotiation. Figuratively speaking, you want to be on the same side of the table as the other party, looking for inventive answers to the problem or dilemma. In a negotiation, find underlying matters, uncover conflicting thoughts, and explore varying interests. One key is to invent as many options as possible before deciding on the best course of action for all parties. In other words, you want to *expand* the pie before you divide it.

Pay attention to the other party. This sounds simple, but it is often left undone. Maintaining eye contact is an easy way to make the other person feel as though you are engaged and listening.

Let go of your own agenda. If you listen carefully to someone for five minutes, they usually tell you – even if it is in passing – about a problem they have. Maybe they like their job, but the commute through traffic is unbearable. Or perhaps they like their job duties, but they do not like the new boss who replaced the manager that brought them into the company. Maybe they were ranked as a top performer, but now they are disappointed with the 3% maximum raises the company gave out last year. Or maybe the person is content with their job generally but would like to spend more time with their family. Focus on their agenda.

Then the issue becomes, how can you help people solve their own problems? One good technique is called *reflexive listening*.

Life Lesson:

How can you help people solve their own problems? One good technique is called reflexive listening.

Reflexive listening means recognizing and comprehending both what a person says and what a person feels, and then conveying this back to the person, paraphrasing in your own words. And you do this without giving your advice – your viewpoint on solving the problem. You simply summarize what they say and then ask them if you have it right. You want to show that you are paying attention and that you have empathy for their situation. Here are some examples:

> Student: "I get it. I need to stop procrastinating and finish my assignments earlier, but I am constantly busy with other things on campus and doing things with my girlfriends. Then I wait until the last minute, and the quality of work is not up to par."

> Professor: "It sounds like you have a busy schedule. Are you saying you are having trouble making your academics the main priority?"

The student will usually say something else to clarify the problem. And the professor will do the reflexive listening technique again. Typically, after a couple of rounds of reflexive listening like this, the student proposes *their own* solution to the problem. The professor rarely needs to *tell* the student the solution. The professor uses reflexive listening and questions to get the student to find the answer for herself. When the student gets to the answer this way, she is more likely to implement the solution because it is *her* idea and not the professor's.

Son: "I really want to go to the Drake concert. And the Migos are going to be the opening act. I saved up all of my money."

Mother: "It sounds like you really want to go to this concert."

Son: "All of my friends from 6th grade are going. You are so unfair."

Mother: "I guess you are feeling upset because you feel I don't trust you? I guess you probably wish you had more freedom?"

Go back and forth until the son is completely understood. Maybe he will propose a solution, such as the parent dropping off and picking up the group of kids immediately after the concert.

Woman in the Relationship: "I value our relationship. However, I feel like you don't put a lot of effort into things like my birthday."

Man in the Relationship: "So, from your point of view, it seems you are feeling unappreciated when it comes to special occasions?"

Woman in the Relationship: "Yes. For example, on our anniversary last month, you took the overtime your job offered you, and we were not even together that evening. I didn't feel special."

Man in the Relationship: "It sounds like you would like me to put more priority on special days and events in our relationship, correct?"

In this example, reflexive listening helps the woman clarify her thinking. The technique helps her understand any underlying emotions. Maybe the man did not previously know that these special occasions were so important. Or perhaps he felt pressured to spend a lot of money on an elaborate celebration, when, all along, the woman would have been totally happy with something simple like a picnic – just spending time with her man.

In summary, you are making tentative statements – soft questions – to show that you are trying to make the other person feel that they are being heard. Resist the impulse to jump in and offer a solution. Guys in relationships are often guilty of this since we generally like to parachute in and "fix" things. Let the person expressing themselves come up with a proposed solution. Maybe the other person just wants to be fully heard and not looking for a solution.

Remember, you have two ears, but only one mouth. Listen more and talk less.

"I like to listen. I have learned a great deal from listening carefully. Most people never listen."

— Ernest Hemingway, Pulitzer Prize-winning novelist, journalist, and sportsman

#DoItNow – What Actions Will You Take as a Result of Reading This Chapter?

1)

2)

3)

CHAPTER EIGHTEEN

THE MAGIC OF MENTORING

"The delicate balance of mentoring someone is not creating them in your own image, but giving them the opportunity to create themselves."

— Steven Spielberg, film director, producer, screenwriter, and billionaire

A mentor is that special person who enables you to see the opportunity for greatness within yourself. A mentee is typically thinking, "What would I have to do to reach my goal, and can I do it?" A mentor helps to empower you to get those questions answered and then pushes you in the direction of your dreams.

A mentoring relationship has dual responsibilities. Both people should bring something to the table. The mentor provides wise counsel based on his or her experience, helping the mentee see what is just over the horizon so he or she can find the best course to their destination. The mentor communicates faith and belief in the mentee.

> **Life Lesson:**
>
> A mentoring relationship has dual responsibilities. Both people should bring something to the table.

The mentee's responsibility is to strongly consider using the mentor's advice. The mentee should also come to each meeting with a specific agenda to make good use of the mentor's time. And the mentee needs to take proactive action to reach their own goals and demonstrate that progress to the mentor.

How can you get started as a mentor? First, figure out who you can best serve. With my background, I provide little value to filmmaking students looking to launch their own careers. However, I can provide a lot of value as a professional mentor to young adults in marketing, public relations, or sales.

Of course, you have to commit the time. It does not necessarily need to be a lot of time, but a consistent cadence is best. I only met with some of my best mentors in corporate America once per quarter. That made sense because they were vice-presidents at Fortune 100 companies. It was my responsibility to put their counsel into action in the intervening three months. On the other hand, when I mentor a high school student, I usually want to meet with them once per month, with maybe a break over the summer.

Think about how you can get positive exposure for your mentee. In corporate America, for example, you can make sure that the mentee gets visibility for the project that he or she worked on. Maybe give the mentee a chance to present the project and results to senior management. When I mentor someone, my mindset is that I want to develop a leader who can pass me up one day. According to John

Maxwell, "The best way a mentor can prepare another leader is to expose him or her to other great people."

Life Lesson:

When I mentor someone, my mindset is that I want to develop a leader who can pass me up one day.

Mentors, sometimes, offer advice. However, you do not want to offer advice in every situation. Often, you will want to listen, ask questions, and eventually *guide* the mentee to find the answers themselves. When you operate this way, the mentees are more likely to implement the agreed-upon course of action.

Throughout our lives and careers, we need strong mentors – and not just our parents. And one mentor is typically not enough. After all, almost everything we know is the knowledge that we acquired from someone else. A diverse set of mentors can help expand our minds in a positive way. We want to surround ourselves with people smarter and more experienced than we are. And, at the same time, you should be a supportive mentor to others. Pay it forward. There is always someone coming behind you.

I have spent countless enjoyable hours mentoring our youth in urban neighborhoods. I won the Salvation Army Man & Youth Award for my work at a Boys & Girls Club in inner-city Baltimore. I did that community service work in Baltimore while in the MBA program at the University of Maryland. They had a banquet where I was supposed to be presented the award. However, the banquet was during the time I was preparing for semester final exams. So, I had to send someone to accept it in my place. Interacting with and encouraging the kids was my reward.

I have also enjoyed being a mentor through programs like the National Black MBA Association's Leaders of Tomorrow Program (LOT). I was especially active as a mentor in my late twenties and early thirties. I co-chaired the program in both Dallas and, subsequently, Atlanta. Professional, educated African Americans, like me, who reached some level of success, must do our part to counter the negative messages that bombard inner-city youth.

Our LOT program in Atlanta grew to nearly one hundred students by 2001. We offered free monthly workshops on a variety of topics to get the students ready for college. We also added an SAT Preparation Course. We must address the disparities that American people of color experience in wealth, health care, and political power. Some African Americans have called for reparations from the U.S. government as compensation for over four hundred years of inequity and discrimination on the North American continent. I personally focused my efforts on programs like LOT, which helped so many young African Americans find a brighter future. First and foremost, I teach that individuals, especially African Americans with major hurdles to overcome, must hold themselves personally responsible. People must take persistent action and be self-reliant and produce results despite the obstacles, including systemic racism. Yes, we need to advocate for economic justice and social justice for all. However, as a mentor, I must also get the mentee to look at themselves in the mirror. Individuals, regardless of ethnicity, cannot allow themselves to fall into a victim mentality.

However, I learned from these young people, too. Interacting with them kept me mentally young and open-minded, which has had long-term benefits for me in terms of strategic thinking, relationships, and friendships. I also had the opportunity to stay in touch with the evolving teenage culture, which eventually helped me when my own children became teenagers.

Life Lesson:

Another benefit of being a mentor is that when you teach something, you learn it better for your own advantage.

Another benefit of being a mentor is that when you teach something, you learn it better for your own advantage. And practice makes perfect. We all know the importance of practice for anything that really matters. We often do not do it because we have this (fake) 'story' that we are too busy to hone our craft. Being a mentor is part of what I call the cycle of excellence that you should use when you want to master any concept: study, practice it yourself, and teach others, including your mentees. Just do it now!

> "My most valued mentor... taught me that failing didn't equate to failure, it just meant you had another shot at getting it right."

> — Jennifer Hedding, Human Resources Executive

166

#DoItNow – What Actions Will You Take as a Result of Reading This Chapter?

1)

2)

3)

CHAPTER NINETEEN

DIVERSITY AND INCLUSION TO SPARK CREATIVITY FOR HIGH PERFORMANCE

"Color is not a human or a personal reality; it is a political reality."

— James Baldwin, novelist, essayist, and activist

As a seven-year-old boy, I intuitively began to build my skills as a person who brings people together – a uniter. When poverty and difficult living conditions forced Joan, my single mother, to frequently make moves between neighborhoods on the North Side of Pittsburgh, I did not want to lose my connections with my friends. From each of our new apartments, I took the initiative to journey up to two miles on foot, taking new friends on what felt like a pilgrimage back to my old hangouts and introducing them around. Because I was having so much fun, I would be gone for many hours until dusk. Unbeknownst to Joan, I made these journeys through the inner city a habit. I eventually got in big trouble when one of my mother's friends saw me on the wrong side of town. I made those trips because I could not accept the idea of giving up that which was left behind, even while I embraced my shifting circumstances.

Eventually, Joan moved us about 25 miles northwest of Pittsburgh to a predominantly white, working-class town called New Brighton. Being a good mother, Joan wanted me to live in a better neighborhood and attend a better school. I was not happy with the move. I was leaving behind my friends and cousins in the city, and I had an extremely hard time, at first, adjusting to being one of the few African American children in the school.

While I was still acclimating to the drastically different environment in New Brighton, my eleven-year-old sixth-grade psyche suffered an enormous jolt one spring evening. Joan revealed, for the first time, that I had been adopted as an infant. I felt so alone and confused. But eventually, with support from my mother and the normal treatment from aunts, uncles, and cousins, I got through it. After all, my cousins did not know that I had been adopted, so they still treated me like any other cousin. Then, fourteen years later, I decided, as a young adult finishing graduate school, to "answer the call" and to search for my heritage – my inherited sense of family identity, values, traditional practices, and culture from preceding generations. I eventually found a white American birth mother who had descended from Lithuanian Jews and a black Kenyan birth father.

Meeting my birth parents and, eventually, my siblings in Europe and Africa was only the beginning. I reverted to my instincts of being a uniter, making multiple trips to England and Kenya to explore my heritage and bring people together into shared acceptance. My international search and the resulting reunions have profoundly affected three families in the United States, England, and Kenya. Another cool part is that all these amazing things happened to me before the age of 30.

If there is one thing I learned through my multicultural American journey, it is that there is *great strength* in our differences. And the United States, while not perfect, is the greatest nation on earth due to the diversity of her citizens.

Life Lesson:

If there is one thing I learned through my multicultural American journey, it is that there is great strength in our differences.

The U.S. is expected to be a so-called "majority-minority" country by 2045, according to the data published by the Brookings Institution in 2018. Given the obvious demographic trends, youthful people of color will be the engine of future growth. People of color will be, by far, the primary source of growth in our working-age population. Most of the growth in new voters will be people of color. And people of color will be the key driver for consumer spending and sustaining a tax base. However, when I talk about America's diversity being a great strength, I am not talking solely about ethnic diversity.

The concept of diversity encompasses acceptance of all the elements that make individuals unique from one another. It means understanding that each person has distinct characteristics and recognizing our individual differences. These differences can be ethnicity, gender, sexual orientation, socioeconomic status, age, physical abilities, veteran status, religious beliefs, political leanings, or other ideologies. Diversity is the consideration and exploration of these differences in a safe, constructive, and nurturing environment.

Life Lesson:

Diversity encompasses acceptance of all the elements that make individuals unique. It means understanding and recognizing our individual differences.

Diversity and inclusion are not the same.

Inclusion is about respecting the differences – the actions and social norms that make certain that people feel welcome. It means understanding each other and moving beyond simple tolerance to embracing and celebrating the rich dimensions of diversity contained within each individual. In the workplace, the Society for Human Resource Management (SHRM) defines inclusion separately from diversity as "the achievement of a work environment in which all individuals are treated fairly and respectfully, have equal access to opportunities and resources, and can contribute fully to the organization's success."

Life Lesson:

Inclusion is about respecting the differences – the actions and social norms that ensure people feel welcome, moving beyond simple tolerance of differences.

An inclusion program may include access, training, and mentoring to enable high-performance organizations and teams of all types. It is about getting the most out of each team member. Inclusion is not only good for large companies; small organizations and individuals can benefit from inclusion. What you voluntarily do, void of coercion, to grow and to win is what inclusion is about. No standards are compromised when you correctly implement an inclusion program.

Some have embraced the acronym IDEA – Inclusion, Diversity, Equity and Access – to promote values and cultures that diminish bias. Equity refers to everyone having the chance to participate and receive fair treatment. Access means that people of all abilities should be incorporated in each initiative.

McKinsey & Company issued a report, *Diversity Wins: How Inclusion Matters* (May 2020), that explains how the business case for inclusion and diversity is more compelling than ever.

In fact, based on the data they collected from more than 1000 companies around the globe, the correlation between diversity on executive teams and the probability of financial outperformance has strengthened over time.

Life Lesson:

The correlation between diversity on executive teams and the probability of financial outperformance has strengthened over time.

McKinsey's 2019 analysis finds that companies in the top quartile for gender diversity on executive teams were 25 percent more likely to have above-average profitability than businesses in the fourth quartile. This number shot up from 21 percent in 2017 and 15 percent in 2014.

Companies with more than 30 percent women executives were more likely to outperform companies where this percentage ranged from 10 to 30.

In the case of ethnic and cultural diversity, McKinsey found, in 2019, that top-quartile companies outperformed those in the fourth one by 36 percent in profitability, slightly up from 33 percent in 2017 and 35 percent in 2014.

However, despite these results and the growing awareness of IDEA as a principle, most companies have made little or no progress on inclusion, diversity, equity, and access. In fact, some have even gone the wrong way. More needs to be done to develop diverse talent to fill management, executive, and board roles. Companies need to do more to enable equal opportunity through impartiality and transparency. For the good of those companies and their shareholders and also for the overall economic strength of our country, the implications for employers are clear: diversity and inclusion must be critical elements of every recruitment and retention strategy.

Another McKinsey & Company report, *The Economic Impact of Closing the Racial Wealth Gap* (August 2019), highlights how the so-called racial wealth gap is not only devastating for African Americans, but also a drag on the overall U.S. economy.

As of 2016, the median white family had more than ten times the wealth of the median African American family. This wealth gap impacts African American communities and the individuals in those communities.

McKinsey found that 65% of the African American population is concentrated in only 16 states. Those states with the most African Americans are generally well below the national averages in economic opportunity, employment, healthcare access, healthcare quality, public health, and broadband access. It is a complicated problem. There is the cumulative impact of over 400 years of systemic racism – policies, constructs, and institutional practices – on this continent. Families have an uphill battle to break the cycle of poverty. There are not enough people of color available as mentors in high positions in corporate America and in our communities. Interactions with the criminal justice system can be fraught with peril for African Americans in some cases – and can potentially lead to depressed lifetime earnings once you acquire an arrest record.

Given the demographic trends described earlier in this chapter, we see the necessity for continued investments in the nation's diverse youth and young adults, as the current population over 50 years old continues to age.

I am optimistic that we can make big progress in these areas over the next five to fifteen years. Moving toward closing the wealth gap over the next ten years – even partially – can add over a trillion dollars per year to the U.S. economy.

As President Barack Obama said, "No matter who you are or what you look like, how you started off, or how and who you love, America is a place where you can write your own destiny."

Former United Nations Secretary-General, Kofi Annan, asserted, "We may have different religions, different languages, different colored skin, but we all belong to one human race." I wholeheartedly agree with Annan's statement.

In the human race, our collective family tree has many branches (ethnicities) with unique characteristics that continue to change over time. Given the many advances in understanding human migration and genetic research over the past 25 years, how is it that we continue to struggle to see that our collective family tree is grounded in the common roots of our ancestors?

We are all *one human race*. There is nothing inherently right or inherently wrong with any group – African American, Asian, Latino, Caucasian, or Native American. To help people understand the details, PBS broadcasted an excellent documentary series that you can check out called *RACE: The Power of an Illusion* (www.racepowerofanillusion.org or at vimeo.com/ondemand/race).

> **Life Lesson:**
>
> We are all one human race.

We have different ethnicities that we can and should celebrate. I love attending ethnic festivals and multicultural events. It is great when people honor their culture.

However, in reality, we are not black, brown, white, yellow, or red, but *merely shades of brown*. We are one human race. "Race" is, at least for now, a real social, historical, cultural, and political construct based largely on outward appearances. And "race" has sometimes been used as a legal construct.

"Race" is *not* a biological construct. It is a myth, scientifically speaking. "Race" has no basis in genetics. Not one characteristic, trait, or even gene differentiates all the humans of one so-called "race" from all the humans of another so-called "race". Scientifically, there are no genetic markers that are in everybody of a distinct "race" and in nobody of some other specific "race". Over the last 400 years, the surface-level differences between humans have sadly become an excuse to institutionalize public policy and individual practices. This has led to socioeconomic, housing, educational, workplace, healthcare, and political disparities.

In 1995, I first arrived at my paternal grandfather's ancestral home in Kenya in East Africa. The specific village is roughly fourteen kilometers west of the town of Kisii and is called Nyakongo. The entire village seemed to be waiting for me, about five hundred people. They were singing and dancing. Everyone was touching my face, skin, beard, and hair since they viewed me as being a *mzungu*, the Kiswahili word for a European or white person. Although I am clearly perceived as African American when in the U.S., it was different there. Light-skinned, wavy-haired Westerners did not come through this remote village every day. In spite of my difference in skin color, I was accepted fully by everyone in the village. Kenyan Africans seem to have almost no notion of racism, despite a history that includes British colonialism. It felt wonderful, and it was truly a wonderful scene.

For many decades in America, the so-called 'one-drop rule' required that anyone with a visually noticeable trace of African, or what was formerly called 'Negro,' heritage was labeled, simply, African American. And if no such visual indicators were apparent, you were still labeled African American, even if you had just one ancestor with that ethnicity. The legal implications were enormous, since this determined whether you could own land, vote, and enjoy the other privileges of full U.S. citizenship. While the one-drop rule is no longer the law, it is still a big part of American culture. For example, the baseball Hall of Famer, Roy Campanella, was Italian but perceived as African American due to his mixed heritage. Former U.S. Secretary of State, Colin Powell, is Scottish, yet culturally, he is viewed as African American.

How might we view each other differently if we truly understood from science that all of our ancient, ancestral *Homo sapiens* parents just happened to evolve in Africa before migrating across the world? I think that, collectively, we would treat each other better if we all knew the fact that we are truly part of the same family tree.

Life Lesson:

We would treat each other better if we all knew the fact that we are truly part of the same family tree.

James King wrote in *The Biology of Race*, "Race is a concept of society that insists there is a genetic significance behind human variations in skin color that transcends outward appearance. However, race has no scientific merit outside of sociological classifications. There are no significant genetic variations within the human species to justify the division of 'races.'"

While the concept of "race" is false, it does have social, cultural, political, and legal implications that we know as racism. All ethnic groups have the unfortunate capability to be racist. Racism is a belief that so-called racial differences produce an inherent superiority of a particular group. And the cycle of racism makes the victimized group more vulnerable to racism – and the offenders more prone to think they are superior and to be drawn to even more racist theories.

However, in today's America, our white brothers and sisters have most of the power. Racism can impact job opportunities for workers and access to business loans for entrepreneurs. Racism can impact where you can rent apartments and where you can own homes. Where you live, including the property you are allowed to buy or rent, can potentially adversely affect your children's education and increase the likelihood they will live in poverty as adults.

I know some African Americans who, unfortunately, are prejudiced against white people. However, African Americans rarely have the power to negatively impact a white person or family in terms of housing, healthcare, jobs, and education.

I do not want *anyone* to be racist. And I always speak up whenever an African American says something racist, even as a so-called joke. Dr. Martin Luther King taught us, "Injustice anywhere is a threat to justice everywhere." In this struggle against racism, we do not have an option of "being Switzerland." Being neutral is not an option. It is not enough to say you are "not racist." We must be *antiracist*, and that means we must take action.

"Someone saying, 'I'm not a racist,' doesn't help the problem," said actor and fitness influencer, Bryce Michael Wood, in the weeks after the May 2020 death of George Floyd. "Simply saying I'm not doing *that* does not save somebody's life. It's like witnessing someone getting jumped and being like, 'Hey, I didn't jump 'em.' But you also just stood there while he or she got jumped. And being an antiracist is like getting involved and being like, 'Break it up. Stop this.'"

A huge reason I stand up to others who do or say racist things is that many people need to be educated to understand that we are all one human race.

Today, the conventional wisdom among scientists is that "race" is only a social construct without biological meaning. Since the Human Genome Project was completed in 2003, it has been very intriguing to look at the discovery that human beings do not have much genetic variation. What are the implications? A white man of French heritage may have more in common – genetically – with a black woman of Nigerian descent than he would with another French man. Skin color is deceptive. Note that there is a huge spectrum of genetic variation *within* the so-called races.

And the concept of "race" is a relatively new idea. The word "race" did not appear in the English language until the early 1500s. Ancient societies, such as the Greeks, grouped people by class and religion, but not according to physical characteristics.

Having said that, I am aware of today's reality in the U.S. and in other places. Not everyone gets this concept of 'one human race' - at least not yet. Thus, the perception of "race" is still a factor in our lives.

As I wrote in my first book, *A Wealth of Family*, despite the ups and downs I experienced in my life, I have an optimistic view on so-called race relations in the world. Prejudice has been in America for over 400 years. Although there will probably always be some prejudice and racism, I believe that things will definitely get better with each generation.

Life Lesson:

Although there will probably always be some prejudice and racism, I believe that things will definitely get better with each generation.

To paraphrase my great Alpha Phi Alpha fraternity brother, Dr. Martin Luther King, we have prejudice and hate because we fear each other. We fear each other because we do not know each other. We do not know each other because we are so often separated from each other. Even so-called "good Christian people" have to agree that one of the most segregated times in America is Sunday morning at 11 A.M. when Blacks and Whites typically go into different buildings to worship the same God using the same Bible. We should, individually, proactively build relationships with people who do not look like us, think like us, worship like us, or act like us.

More education and diverse experiences can eradicate racism and create world citizens. I am proud of my heritage as an African American. I also learned to view myself as a world citizen. I am no longer limited by ethnicity, religion, nationality, or political ideology. During my travels to all seven continents, I learned to embrace diverse cultures, ideas, and ethnic groups. With this perspective, it is easy to see that the two-way racism between Blacks and Whites in America is the result of ignorance.

Furthermore, discord within the African American community, between light-skinned and dark-skinned people, also known as colorism, is misguided. Ethnic group conflicts over politics like those in Kenya are tragic and self-defeating. Disputes over lineage and ethnicity that lead to war, like those in Bosnia and Herzegovina, are even more irrational. Japanese have fought Koreans, Indians have fought with Pakistanis, and the list goes on. When we realize that all people are citizens of the world and then begin to truly value diverse cultures, ideas, and backgrounds, the world becomes less dangerous, and people suffer less.

We can initiate firm inroads against racism, tribalism, and infighting through education and awareness. For example, education about our own history now allows African Americans to take pride in our great inventors, writers, physicians, and statesmen. I want to encourage African Americans, often oppressed for over four hundred years but now more educated than ever on our own history, to take pride in our influence on world culture.

Right or wrong, the United States has more influence than any other country on the world's popular culture, including music, dance, fashion, and movies. I personally saw this influence during my various travels in Africa, Asia, Australia, Europe, and South America. In my opinion, African Americans do the most to set the overall tempo for pop culture in the United States. African Americans gave the world jazz, blues, gospel, funk, rap, and hip-hop. Elements of African American culture are then assimilated into "America's culture," and then American culture propagates across the world. This phenomenon is monumental, and African Americans often receive little credit for it.

Leveraging my books, family heritage, and career experiences, I give speaking engagements and provide training for professional organizations, companies, and universities on the topics of diversity, multiculturalism, and inclusion. Every time I lead such training, I realize more and more that we must move beyond basic tolerance to a full embrace of our differences. This is a big part of being antiracist. Only when this occurs can an individual or organization cope with the changes that are coming in the 2020s and beyond. I always challenge the audience to proactively build relationships with people "who do not look like you, think like you, worship like you, or act like you." I challenge everyone, regardless of their ethnicity, to be antiracist, not just non-racist. As Elie Wiesel asserted, "Neutrality helps the oppressor, never the victim. Silence encourages the tormentor, never the tormented. Sometimes we must interfere."

Life Lesson:

We must move beyond basic tolerance to a full embrace of our differences. This is a crucial part of being antiracist and thriving in the 2020s and beyond.

By investing in awareness around the issues of diversity, multiculturalism, and inclusion, organizations can improve employee relations, better serve their customers, and become more innovative by fully leveraging the talents and experiences of every team member. Embrace diversity. Just do it now!

> "Diversity is being invited to the party;
> inclusion is being asked to dance."

— Verná Myers, VP of Inclusion Strategy at Netflix

#DoItNow – What Actions Will You Take as a Result of Reading This Chapter?
1)
2)
3)

CHAPTER TWENTY

THE IMPACT OF HATERS, BOTH REAL AND IMAGINED

"It is in the character of very few men to honor without envy a friend who has prospered."

— Aeschylus, ancient Greek playwright, and poet

A 'hater' is very informally defined as a person who thrives on showing hate toward, criticizing, or belittling other people or things, usually unfairly. A hater cannot be glad about another person's success. The hater just wants to knock the other person off a figurative pedestal. Figuratively speaking, the hater drinks 'Haterade' and drowns himself or herself in over-the-top negativity.

Do not be a hater. When others succeed, cheer them on. Be positive, whether the other person hated on you or not. Very few things in life are a zero-sum game. In other words, a colleague, competitor, or friend can be successful, and you can climb toward and eventually reach your own dreams, as well.

> **Life Lesson:**
>
> Do not be a hater. When others succeed, cheer them on. Be positive, whether the other person hated on you or not.

How do you handle it when haters target you?

You can follow the advice of comedienne and talk show host, Ellen DeGeneres, who was quoted as saying, "Normally, I try not to pay attention to my haters, but this time I'd like to talk about it because my haters are my motivators."

Singer and actress, Kesha, was quoted as follows, "Of course there are certain things that get to me, but I try and lead by example and show people that, especially with haters, you should just ignore them."

On the Internet, you are going to encounter trolls. In the era of social media, haters – both real and imagined – can sometimes be tough to ignore. But remember that you get to calculate your own self-worth. There is no need to rely on haters or friends, or anyone else for validation.

How do we determine our own self-worth? How are identities typically formed? I will share a story from my childhood and its impact, as an example.

I grew up with a single mom in inner-city Pittsburgh. As a kid, I grew uncomfortable with being poor—that is, poor by American standards. I struggled being poor partly because of needs and wants and partly because of pride. When I was six years old, an incident that hurt my fragile pride evolved from a simple trip to the grocery store with one of my friends. My friend's family sent him to get two small jars of baby food for his younger sibling. I remember each jar costing about twenty-nine cents back then. On the way home, we stopped for some reason, and he asked me to hold the bag with the baby food inside. While we were waiting, the brown paper bag slipped out of my clumsy hand. The two jars broke. My friend said, "I can't show up at home without this baby food. My momma will kill me." So, I went to my mother for the fifty-eight cents, but she did not have it. I was embarrassed to have to tell my friend that I would have to give him and his mother the fifty-eight cents the following week. In the aftermath of those events, my *perception* was that my status diminished in the eyes of the local haters – the other kids in the projects. From then on, I had an acute awareness of money and the fact that my family lacked it. I knew I would have to be smart in school and work hard if I wanted to prosper.

You might be thinking, "That's great; you decided to focus on academics and hard work. What's the problem?" But we need to go through the details of how this incident shaped my identity.

What I 'decided' was wrong with me in that moment was basically, *I am poor*. My pride was wounded. And I felt that I was not good enough because my family lacked money.

I had this feeling, even though I have no memory of anyone verbally abusing me. In this case, the haters were imagined, not real.

After I processed those thoughts and feelings, as well as any 6-year-old can, I took on a new way of being. In that moment, what I *decided* to be was essentially, "I must be super smart in school and be hardworking to get out of poverty." Even though I now understand that it was just a story I told myself, that is how I felt then and for years thereafter.

By the time I was in 10th grade, I planned on a career as a history teacher or a sportswriter. I loved history, and I loved sports. I wrote a letter to the University of Pittsburgh journalism department and asked what it took to be a sportswriter. I received an encouraging return letter and a signed copy of an awesome book about baseball, written by one of Pitt's professors. I quickly consumed every word in the book. I was poised to be a sports journalist.

However, near the end of 10th grade, I read an article that discussed various majors and careers. I noticed that among four-year degrees, the highest starting salaries were for engineering majors. The salaries for teachers and journalists lagged behind the salaries for engineers. The article noted that an engineer typically enjoyed and excelled in math and the sciences.

At that time, I got almost all A's in all my school courses. I believed I could handle any academic major in college if I studied hard. I liked math and science well enough, so I decided I would go to college to study engineering just to lift myself out of poverty more quickly.

As a result of this focus, I became a high school valedictorian and earned a Bachelor of Science in Electrical Engineering. However, the impact of living out my way of being, which developed when I was only 6 years old, was that I *decided* to choose a limiting identity. I *decided* that I was *just* the smart, hard-working kid (now an engineer) and not the person who brings creativity, especially to social situations. I got caught up in the stereotype of many engineers. This limiting belief stayed with me throughout high school and through my undergraduate years. I started to tell myself stories that became self-fulfilling prophecies, such as: "I am not going to be able to come up with anything creative for my girlfriend on Valentine's Day," or maybe "I am not going to be able to come up with a creative way to sell my project proposal at work, I am just the engineer."

I was 23 years old when I finally fully put to death this arbitrary ceiling on my performance. At that point, I decided I can be creative *and* also a smart engineer. The two are not mutually exclusive. Be careful to make sure that the incidents that happened to you between ages four and 18 do not negatively impact your identity for the *rest of your life*. You can choose your way of being in spite of any haters – real or imagined.

Life Lesson:

Be careful to make sure that the incidents that happened to you between ages four and 18 do not negatively impact your identity for the rest of your life.

In summary, you can ignore your haters – both real and imagined – or you can let your haters be your motivators, allowing their negativity to be the fuel that powers you forward. Whichever inspires you to greatness, just do it now!

> "Haters will broadcast your failure
> but whisper your success."
>
> — Drake, rapper, singer, actor, and entrepreneur

188

#DoItNow – What Actions Will You Take as a Result of Reading This Chapter?
1)
2)
3)

CHAPTER TWENTY-ONE

EXCUSES ARE THE TOOLS OF INCOMPETENCE

"I have nothing in common with lazy people who blame others for their lack of success. Great things come from hard work and perseverance. No excuses."

— Kobe Bryant, 5-time NBA Champion

Microsoft founder and billionaire, Bill Gates, is quoted as saying, "You can make money and you can make excuses, but you can never make money out of excuses."

During my college days, when I was pledging my fraternity, I learned the following widely used declaration about explanations and justifications: "Excuses are the tools of incompetence, which build monuments to nothing. Those who specialize in them seldom succeed in anything at all."

You cannot deposit excuses in your bank account. Excuses may, perhaps, earn you pity, but that is about it. Your triumph only comes when your dreams grow larger than your fears and weak excuses.

Instead of manufacturing excuses, we need to manufacture good habits.

Life Lesson:

Excuses are the tools of incompetence, which build monuments to nothing. Those who specialize in them seldom succeed in anything at all.

Demonstrate reliability and integrity. Do what you say you are going to do. And the most important person you need to be truthful with is yourself. Train your mind – specifically your subconscious mind – to always do what you say you are going to do.

As you manufacture good habits, know that only a new habit can overpower another habit. That happens through practice and repetition. When you become good at the task, it is natural to enjoy doing it.

In other words, self-discipline, demonstrated by performing a task repeatedly, is what makes a desirable habit your servant, instead of your master. Be consistent. Usually, a new habit takes at least 30 days to really stick. And if you are a leader of a team, know that your team is watching you to see if you are consistent. Folks will do what you do and not what you say.

In the book, *Outliers*, author, Malcolm Gladwell, says that it typically takes roughly 10,000 hours of practice to achieve mastery in a field. Look at the people who are elite at what they do. Hockey great, Sidney Crosby, spent thousands of hours shooting pucks as he was growing up. He not only practiced shooting while on the ice, but he also even had a net in his basement at home. From 1960 to 1964,

The Beatles performed live in Hamburg, Germany, over 1200 times. It was not easy, and the crowds were sometimes difficult. However, they accumulated so much performing time. From then on, The Beatles were unstoppable.

Another irresistible force in the music industry is Beyoncé. She has spent *over 20 years* on the music scene, and she will perform, rain or shine. Once, she even performed at the Grammy Awards while she was already far into her pregnancy. Nothing seems to stop her from perfecting her craft, earning money, and growing her brand.

Bill Gates, who grew up in a privileged family and environment, got access to computers in the late 1960s and early 1970s. His prep school had a computer, which was extremely rare back then. Gates got in *years* of computer programming as a teenager, which prepared him to launch Microsoft by 1975. Meanwhile, some of us want to quickly give up on our dreams if we are not wildly successful in the first month.

Life Lesson:

Some of us want to quickly give up on our dreams if we are not wildly successful in the first month.

Once we develop good habits, we need persistence, which is defined as a firm or obstinate continuance in a course of action in spite of difficulty or opposition. Persistence itself is actually a habit. You need to know that 'not quitting' is not the same as taking persistent action. And persistent action is easier once fear has been eradicated (we deal with fear and confidence in Chapter Twenty-Two).

All excuses boil down to one of the following: Not enough time. Not enough money. Not enough support. Not enough ability. And they are *never really true* when it comes to realizing your goals, especially if you are persistent. I am not saying that time, money, support, and ability are not important; I am saying that if you are committed to your goals, you can find a way eventually.

Life Lesson:

All excuses boil down to one of the following: Not enough time. Not enough money. Not enough support. Not enough ability – all not true with enough persistence.

The story of how I reunited with my biological parents is a prime example of intense persistence. I was adopted as an infant. I found my biological mother and her family in Europe when I was in my mid-20s. In 1994, I wanted to find my family on my biological father's side in Kenya. All I knew about my biological father was his name. I talked to a few people, and they gave me the likely ethnic group, which is Kisii. At the time, there were about two million Kisii people in Kenya. So, I figured, what the heck. At least, the number is two million and not 10 million. So, I flew to Nairobi on New Year's Eve, 1994, to ramp up my search.

I only knew one person from Nairobi named Fatma; I had met her previously when she visited friends in the U.S., and she spoke English and Kiswahili. One of the initial things we did was to call everyone in the Nairobi phone book that had my Kenyan family name of

Omwenga. However, the phone directories were several years old, so we had no luck.

I spent Sunday, January 1, 1995, on photo safari and rural western Kenya. Government buildings were closed on Sunday in Nairobi, so I did not feel the photo safari was impeding my search. However, it turned out Monday, January 2nd was a bank holiday, so the government buildings were closed again. I did manage to visit the offices of the *Daily Nation*, the leading East African newspaper. I decided to place an ad that would run on Wednesday, January 4, as I had missed the deadline for Tuesday.

On Tuesday morning, the search began in earnest. I went to see Dr. Zachary Onyonka. I had heard that Dr. Onyonka was a Kisii who was said to have gone to school in Syracuse, New York, in the mid-1960s. I felt that he was our best lead since he was in America at the same time as my biological father. However, Dr. Onyonka, whose official title was Minister for Research, Technical Training, and Technology, was a busy member of the Kenyan Cabinet and was not in his office. His secretary was gracious and told us that Dr. Onyonka would be back at four o'clock that afternoon. We asked her to help us look for the two Omwengas whom we heard worked in the Treasury Building. After forty-five minutes of calls, she could not locate them.

Things that we took for granted in the United States, such as online phone directories, email, and phone calls that go through instantly, were scarce in Kenya in 1995. The helpful secretary referred us to another government employee, Dr. I. A. Onyango, also a Kisii. He was very helpful, even though we went to see him with no appointment. He spent so much time trying to help us that I wondered what he was supposed to be doing in terms of his actual job duties.

Dr. Onyango's friendly secretary, Winnie, agreed to help us put in inquiries to a couple of well-connected Kisii men that she knew. The names we were given were Henderson Magare and Nyang'au Omwenga.

We then visited the U.S. Embassy in Nairobi, the eventual site of the August 1998 terrorist bombing. The consular officer tried to help us, but the embassy only kept visa records for one year from travel. Thus, my biological father's travel records from the 1960s were not available.

I was chasing about 14 different leads. By now, it was Wednesday morning, my last full day in Africa before heading home to the U.S. the next morning so I could get back to work.

After that, there was definitely a sense of urgency. The ad had run in the *Daily Nation* newspaper on Wednesday as planned. Later, we, again, went to see Dr. Zachary Onyonka. We never did get to meet him despite multiple visits to his office, and he never responded to the detailed note that we left for him on Tuesday. What I had believed to be our best lead bore no fruit.

By sunset, Wednesday, our last night in Kenya, the leads from Winnie, Dr. Onyango's friendly secretary, and the newspaper ad began to converge. When I returned to the hotel, I saw a note that said a Robert Nyamwaro Omwenga had stopped by while we were out. It turns out that he is my uncle. By the time I had departed the next morning, I had met one of my Kenyan sisters and two uncles. I was ecstatic!

I subsequently went to Kenya four more times over the next six years. Not only did I meet my biological father and my other Kenyan siblings, but I also eventually went to my family's village in rural western Kenya, where I was warmly welcomed by the villagers. I was able to see my grandmother on two different trips. No excuses – persistence paid off.

I learned that belief does not come from success. Success actually comes from belief. The correct order is BE, then DO, then HAVE. To accomplish something, you must first believe that it can be done. Because of my beliefs, I am persistent.

If you really want to get it done, find a way to do it now. If your excuse is that you do not have time, then prioritize the tasks that will get you financial freedom so that you can effectively buy back your time. If your excuse is that you do not have the knowledge, use Google and YouTube to find free training on almost any topic. If your excuse is that you do not have support, then support yourself and just do it anyway. If your excuse is that you have a lot going against you, remember that you have a lot going for you, as well. Have an attitude of gratitude.

Life Lesson:

Difficulty of a task is no excuse. Just draw inspiration from human history.

The difficulty of a task is no excuse. Just draw inspiration from human history. Building Stonehenge in England was not effortless. The Great Pyramid of Giza in Egypt was not easy to erect thousands of years ago. Think of the complexity, strain, and required bravery needed to enable a successful D-Day invasion during World War II.

Imagine the trials and tribulations experienced by Martin Luther King, Jr., John Lewis, and thousands of others that labored in the American civil rights movement. In the 21st century, think of the difficulty in building the 163-story Burj Khalifa in Dubai, the tallest building in the world since 2009 at 2,717 feet, just over half a mile. Or the astonishing expansion of mobile phone networks globally, providing more inclusivity than any technology in history, improving the livelihoods of billions of people. If your goal is too hard, or you are too tired, or it is not the right time, just do it anyway!

"Those who are successful overcome their fears and take action. Those who aren't submit to their fears and live with regrets."

— Jay-Z, rapper, record executive,
and billionaire entrepreneur

#DoItNow – What Actions Will You Take as a Result of Reading This Chapter?
1)
2)
3)

CHAPTER TWENTY-TWO

THE ART OF EXTRAORDINARY CONFIDENCE

---

*"Pressure is what you feel when you
are not prepared to do your job."*

— Chuck Noll, former Pittsburgh Steelers
Coach and 4-time Super Bowl Champion

Confidence is having faith in yourself and knowing that you add value to people and organizations. If you exude confidence as a leader, then people are more likely to follow you. Confidence is generally attractive to people that you might want to date. And confidence also invites success by attracting the people and conditions that lead to achievement.

Be prepared, and you will be confident. I call it the luck of the prepared. The Roman philosopher, Seneca, observed, "Luck is when opportunity meets preparation."

Confidence starts with choosing to have the right mindset, even before the confidence is there. Remember, we can control the thoughts in our conscious mind. As civil rights icon and politician,

Jesse Jackson, stated, "If my mind can conceive it, and my heart can believe it, then I can achieve it."

Life Lesson:

Confidence starts with choosing to have the right mindset, even before the confidence is there.

Be mindful of perceptions. As your skills and leadership abilities grow, you want to be perceived as being confident – not perceived as being arrogant. In day-to-day interactions, there is no need to toot your own horn. Let other people, such as professors, bosses, and clients, brag about your exploits.

How can you enhance your confidence? One place to start is with your grooming and appearance, the first impressions covered in Chapter Fifteen. Are you dressed appropriately for today's event? Is your shirt ironed? Is your breath fresh? I was taught in corporate America to dress for the job you want, not the job you have. Pro Football Hall of Famer, Deion Sanders, puts it this way, "If you look good, you feel good. If you feel good, you play good. If you play good, they pay good."

On a related note, you want to make sure you exercise regularly. Exercise helps your appearance, gives you the physical confidence and the energy to conquer the world, or at least your own to-do list, and helps you stay healthy.

You also want to eradicate negative thinking, which can cause you to lose confidence. The way to do that is simple. Use your conscious mind to replace the negative thought with a positive thought. One way to do this is to ask yourself, "What would I say to a friend who is dealing with this issue?" For example, if you have the negative thought of, "I'll never get rid of the 20 pounds I need to lose in order to fit my favorite clothes", then give yourself the positive thought of, "I can create a specific plan based on healthy eating and exercise so that I can have the body I desire." Over time, the positive thinking will lead to positive outcomes. Soon, you will get in the habit of doing it all the time. And when you wipe out negative thinking, then negative things will not come out of your mouth.

Life Lesson:

You also want to eradicate negative thinking, which can cause you to lose confidence. Use your conscious mind to replace the negative thought with a positive thought.

Once you improve your positive thinking, do positive things. The correct order is BE, then DO, then HAVE. It starts with a way of being, which allows you to take the right actions so that you will have the result. Talk to people consistently based on your positive mental attitude, and your confidence will flourish.

One way I improved my confidence as a young professional was to increase my academic and technical skills. As an undergraduate, I secured four consecutive summer internships in corporate America by being part of an organization called INROADS. INROADS, Inc. is a national organization designed to groom talented Hispanic, African American, and Native American youth for positions of leadership in corporate America and in their communities. It has affiliates across

America. The organization builds bridges between corporate America and the communities of color. One of the things the INROADS staff drilled into us back then was the idea of "technical competence". They did not mean that everyone needs to major in engineering. The point is that our confidence will increase in the workplace and in our entrepreneurial endeavors if we master knowledge, behaviors, and skills unique to a particular line of business, profession, or academic area.

What is another way to build your confidence? When you *know* that you *know* that you always honor your commitments (especially to yourself), your self-confidence will be off the charts. This can be achieved by developing the positive habit of doing the tasks you say you are going to do – and doing them every single time. And you can start with minor tasks and commitments to build this confidence through habits. Chapter Five discusses habits in detail.

After all, who wants to wake up every morning needing to 'overcome fear' when it comes to getting important tasks done? No one does. The idea is to *eradicate* fear completely. When you honor the commitments you made to yourself, it becomes a successful habit. Only a new, good habit can replace a bad habit. You can start with writing down minor easy tasks and creating the habit of doing them on time without fail. I am mindful of my thoughts. The inside world (my thoughts) gives me the confidence to create the outside world (business, wealth, fun, and health).

Although we can only think of one thing at a time in our conscious mind, we, fortunately, can control that thought. As personal development author, Brian Tracy, explains, "Your conscious mind commands and your subconscious mind obeys. Your subconscious mind is an unquestioning servant that works day and night to make your behavior fit a pattern consistent with your emotionalized thoughts, hopes, and desires. Your subconscious mind grows either flowers or weeds in the garden of your life, whichever you plant by the mental equivalents you create."

Before you know it, you have moved on from small tasks and are now confidently *completing* a so-called 'bigger' task about which you were previously experiencing feelings of fear, which causes procrastination. In Chapter Two, we covered the concept of your Definite Major Purpose (DMP). Focus on that overarching goal and embrace the bigger picture to get the motivation to take persistent action and do it now.

Maybe you are fearful about committing to working out regularly every week to help prevent the onset of diabetes. In spite of the doctor's warnings about your recent lab results, you have a fear of change, which can leave you stagnant. The motivation you might want to embrace is longevity so you can be there for your family.

Maybe you are fearful about your ability to manage your diet to get to your target healthy weight. The fear you want to eliminate is your perception that you are not good enough. Perhaps the extra motivation you need comes from imagining how you will look on the beach during the vacation that you have already booked for five months from now.

Possibly, you are staying in a dating relationship that you know is bad for you. Maybe there is verbal or emotional abuse in your current relationship. It could be that you want to eliminate the fear of feeling lonely. Your motivation may come from creating the possibility of making room in your life for a new relationship based on love, trust, and acceptance.

Maybe you are in corporate America, and you want to change departments to have new responsibilities. You want to eradicate the fear of uncertainty that can prevent you from trying new things. A higher position and more compensation may be your motivation to stop procrastinating.

Perhaps you are nervous about starting a part-time entrepreneurial venture because you fear failure. However, your burning desire to retire 15 years early with time freedom and financial freedom motivates you to take persistent action.

Or maybe the fear you are experiencing is related to making the 10 sales calls per day that you know will grow your business. Eradicate the fear of rejection. The motivation may come from whatever you want to do with the profits you earn. For example, you may want to pay off student loan debt for yourself or reduce the need for any student loans for your children.

Your subconscious mind cannot discern between small/easy tasks and big/hard tasks. Create a habit of actually doing everything you write down, and that eradicates the fear and builds extraordinary confidence. Habits are covered in Chapter Five.

Life Lesson:

Create a habit of actually doing everything you write down and that eradicates the fear and builds extraordinary confidence.

Muhammad Ali bragged, "I am the greatest; I said that even before I knew I was."

I control my thoughts. You can also. Answer the door with confidence when opportunity knocks. Just do it now!

"It is better to be prepared for an opportunity and not have one than to have an opportunity and not be prepared."

— Whitney M. Young, Jr., civil rights leader and former Executive Director of National Urban League

#DoItNow – What Actions Will You Take as a Result of Reading This Chapter?
1)
2)
3)

CHAPTER TWENTY-THREE

ENTHUSIASM

"Force yourself to act enthusiastic, and you'll become more enthusiastic."

— Frank Bettger, author, lecturer, and former Major League Baseball player

Enthusiasm is contagious. Therefore, you want to spend most of your time around energetic people who have a passion for their lives and careers. And as a leader, people are more likely to follow you if you are enthusiastic. In a team environment, you can spread your enthusiasm to others, which can have great benefits for everyone involved. Enthusiasm can often save the day when things go wrong.

Enthusiasm means that you are highly engaged in the things that you do and that you enjoy those things. Possessing and radiating enthusiasm is a learned skill. You want to be very intentional about your level of enthusiasm. When you practice this skill consistently, people will think it is your natural disposition.

How can you practice enthusiasm? When you are about to do something, just tell yourself to be *10 times more excited*. I do this when I am about to meet with potential clients. It gets me to smile and makes my energy surge.

> **Life Lesson:**
>
> Possessing and radiating enthusiasm is a learned skill. You want to be very intentional about your level of enthusiasm. Shoot for 10X more excited!

However, you cannot be enthusiastic about everything. Therefore, you must ruthlessly prioritize. You only get 168 hours each week, so you want to focus on projects that inspire instead of drain.

To find that inspiration, you first need knowledge of the project or product. Next, you need belief. It is impractical to be enthusiastic without belief.

After discovering the things that you can be truly enthusiastic about, and you make enthusiasm a habit, then that habit can crush any tendency for procrastination. Hockey Hall of Famer, Wayne Gretzky, said, "Procrastination is one of the most common and deadliest of diseases, and its toll on success and happiness is heavy."

On a related note, be careful about the things that can drain your enthusiasm. Maintaining your health is essential to maintaining your enthusiasm. Make sure you get enough sleep. Even if you are young and strong, you are not invincible. Getting suboptimal sleep over a long period of time can lead to some severe health problems. And your mood suffers as well, leaving you unable to generate your best level of enthusiasm.

You want to make sure you eat well. A healthy diet is a big factor in a healthy lifestyle, giving you the energy to maintain your enthusiasm. However, many Americans – maybe even you -- need help to move toward a healthier lifestyle. Some of the biggest healthcare challenges we face in America is the need to end diabetes, heart disease, and obesity.

Ending these menaces to our long-term health require significant changes in public awareness and perception, in our politics, and ultimately in policy and legislation. Some of the factors that hinder progress are:

- Perceived cost of healthy foods
- Lack of availability of healthy foods in some neighborhoods
- Increased restaurant serving portions
- Abundance of unhealthy fast foods and other convenience foods
- Sedentary lifestyles

Life is remarkably busy for most people. Most families have both parents working, making it difficult to make homemade meals for the children and the family. It is even more challenging for single-parent households. This lack of time often leads to more eating out or less healthy convenience foods that probably contain more sugar, salt, and fat.

As a nation, we live more sedentary lifestyles. Parents have the primary responsibility to teach their kids about healthy eating and lifestyles. All the stakeholders – corporate America, parents, government agencies, healthcare companies, and the food industry – should recommit themselves to enabling healthier diets and lifestyles.

This will provide a healthy jolt to the enthusiasm and productivity of most Americans. I, for one, can get 10 times more excited about that.

***

Once I started dating my wife, Nikki, I eventually wanted to get to know her parents. Nikki and I were living in Atlanta, while her parents lived in Huntsville, Alabama. When I first met Nikki's mom, Vanona, in March 2000, I greeted Vanona with enthusiasm with a big hug and a kiss on the cheek. Vanona had previously been very, extremely tough on all of Nikki's boyfriends in the past. Nikki and the rest of her family expected more of the same when it was time to meet me. Fortunately, my enthusiasm and actions won Vanona over immediately, and we continued to get along fine after that. Similarly, I always had a good relationship with her father, Lenel.

Fast forward to Fall 2000, as the country was about to have a presidential election on November 7th. My beloved Pittsburgh Steelers were scheduled to play in Nashville against the Tennessee Titans on Sunday, November 5th. Since I was still building a relationship with Nikki's parents, I came up with an idea a few weeks before the game. Since Nashville is only roughly 100 miles north of Huntsville, we could spend the weekend in Huntsville and then drive up to the game on Sunday morning.

Of course, if you are enthusiastically looking to impress the people who are likely to be your future in-laws, you must get good seats. I was running out of time, so I searched online, found, and purchased four perfect tickets. The tickets were $250 each, but I felt that spending $1000 to cap a nice weekend with Nikki's parents would be worth it in this case.

A few days before the game, while still in Atlanta, I had a tire blow out on my 1998 BMW M3 sedan. I loved that car back then – a cool, fast black sports car with four doors – but I was having a lot of problems with my tires. They consistently wore unevenly, causing occasional flats and the purchase of many replacement tires. Because the M3 is a sports car – a driving machine – it was equipped with low profile tires, giving the car lots of responsiveness on curvy roads. I appreciated that, but low-profile tires are much more vulnerable to damage from the road. And these tires were expensive, costing $300 each for the tires and installation. When you have a blowout, you cannot replace just one tire. You either replace both front tires or both rear tires as appropriate so that they can wear evenly.

I took my car to the shop, but they did not have my special low-profile tire in stock. They called around but had no luck. The shop said they could order new tires, and they would be in by Monday – which would be after my weekend in Huntsville.

I did not like this option, but I had little choice. So, I had them put on the spare, and Nikki and I took off on the three-hour drive to Huntsville on that Friday. We did not take Nikki's car because it only had two doors, and it would not have been comfortable for her parents riding in the back seat to Nashville.

After a nice time in Huntsville on Friday and Saturday, the four of us jumped in my car on Sunday morning to head to the football game. I was excited to see the game, and I was secretly hoping to turn Vanona into a Steelers fan. I even gave her a Steelers jersey.

We crossed the state line into Tennessee. We were cruising northbound on I-65. I was in the far-left lane, probably going a little faster than the speed limit. All of a sudden – pop! I knew instantly that a tire had blown out. I held the steering wheel steady with both hands and then carefully moved three or four lanes to the right so I could safely get off the highway without causing an accident. It was not easy. Once we were stopped safely on the side of the road, I just put my head on the steering wheel in total disgust.

Lenel said, "Hey, you did a great job getting us off the road safely. It's no problem; we'll make it to the game. Let's just put on the spare. I will help you."

I did not look up. Finally, after an awfully long pause, I told Lenel and Vanona the story of why I had no spare tire. I was disappointed and embarrassed, and I felt that I had let them down. However, they were totally understanding and supportive because I had put so much effort, real enthusiasm, into making the weekend happen.

So, we called a tow truck, and after a long wait, we had the M3 taken to the closest BMW dealer, which was back in Alabama. Of course, their service department was closed on Sunday. So, we left my car at the dealer and eventually found a way to rent a car. After spending all this time, it was clear we were not going to make it to the game. So, we drove the rental car back to Huntsville.

At this point, I am out of $1000 for the tickets and maybe another $700 for tires I would need, including installation. We watched the fourth quarter from a sports bar. To add insult to injury, my Steelers lost the game to the Titans, 9-7.

Nikki and I drove the rental car back to Atlanta. On Monday, I called the dealer in Alabama, and they said that the car would be ready by Tuesday – and by the way, I also needed a new rim. It turns out one of my wheels had a small hairline crack. As a result of that, the tire would slowly lose air and eventually cause uneven wear on all the tires. Problem identified. This is why I was burning through so much cash for new low-profile tires.

I voted in the election on Tuesday in Atlanta; then I drove the rental car three hours back to the dealer north of Huntsville to get my own vehicle. That same night, I listened to the election returns, which turned out to be inconclusive at that point in the George W. Bush vs. Al Gore contest – while driving my car for three hours back to Atlanta.

In the end, my enthusiasm kept the weekend from being a total loss. That haphazard trip actually brought me closer together with Nikki's parents.

So, what did I learn, if nothing else? After that incident, I found TireRack.com as a way to save money on tires. More importantly, I was reminded that I should always put my "Six P's" in action – *proper prior planning promotes peak performance!*

Life Lesson:

You must take action to jump start your enthusiasm. Think about how you might utilize something you have a passion for as a catalyst to become more enthusiastic.

Finally, the episode reaffirmed to me that you must take action to jump start your enthusiasm. Think about how you might utilize something you have a passion for – such as football or family time – as a catalyst to become more enthusiastic. Whatever you are looking to achieve, enthusiastically get started today. Just do it now!

"Wherever you go, go with all your heart."

— Confucius, ancient Chinese philosopher

#DoItNow – What Actions Will You Take as a Result of Reading This Chapter?
1)
2)
3)

CHAPTER TWENTY-FOUR

UNDER PROMISE, OVER DELIVER

"Under Promise, Over Deliver."

— Tom Peters, bestselling author of *In Search of Excellence*

Make sure your word is your bond. In your social life, corporate career, and your entrepreneurial endeavors, always deliver what you promise.

The significance of "under promise and over deliver" is a service approach where providers strive for excellent customer service and satisfaction by doing more than they say they will, exceeding customer expectations. This method works, for example, when a vendor company promises something to another company that is their client.

And I would contend that "under promise and over deliver" is a mindset that is even more important for you as an individual. When you commit something to an internal co-worker, your individual credibility is on the line. When you make a promise to a customer, your individual standing is on the line, at least as much as that of your company. And when you make an agreement in your personal life, the perception of your personal brand is at stake.

Life Lesson:

"Under promise and over deliver" is a mindset that is even more important for you as an individual than for your company. Do what you say you are going to do.

Do what you say you are going to do. It is about expectation management. Be ten minutes early for meetings so that others are not waiting. Be reliable. If you promise a price for your goods and services, honor that price for the duration of the quoted period.

Of course, I understand that no one is perfect. Sometimes, things do go wrong that are beyond your control. However, those instances should be exceedingly rare. And when they do happen, you should already have a strong track record and a reputation for overdelivering.

There is one caveat to this service strategy. In a competitive situation, when you are submitting a bid to win new business from a client or customer, you may want to *slightly* Under Promise, Over Deliver. In other words, if you are too conservative and do not promise enough to meet client needs, you will not win the contract.

If you are known for *under-promising and over-delivering*, it will become part of your personal brand. You do not even have to say those five words. You simply need to just do it now.

> **Life Lesson:**
>
> If you are known for under promising and over delivering, it will become part of your personal brand.

In general, one definition of a brand is a person's *perception* of a product, service, experience, or organization.

Before we look at personal branding, let us examine a few examples from corporate America to get perspective. The Tesla brand represents luxury and style in the electric vehicle marketplace. The brand promise is that one can save the world through reduced emissions and still drive a fast car and look cool doing it. Tesla automobiles are perceived differently than the Toyota Prius, which primarily focuses on fuel economy and reduced emissions.

Another successful branding example is Grubhub. They revolutionized the experience of ordering takeout food. Everything is handled in the app, which dramatically improves order accuracy. Another part of the brand promise is the wide selection of restaurant menus you can access. The old idea of calling someone and talking to them to order your food seems to be an antiquated approach in the 2020s.

Delta Air Lines won multiple prestigious awards in recent years for superior customer experience. The evaluators looked at how customers rated their overall flight experience, as well as seat comfort, cabin service, food and beverage, entertainment, and Wi-Fi. It is all about client experience. For example, if the in-flight movie does not work, a Delta employee proactively approaches the customer or customers that were impacted. In many cases, the employee has a tablet, and the employee shows the customer that extra frequent flyer miles have *already* been placed in their account. The company is known to often do this whether you complain about the movie or other inconvenience or not. How do you feel, as a customer, about Delta's brand promise when they take care of you like this? It is like an upgrade to first class.

When it comes to building your personal brand, not everyone can be Oprah or Beyoncé – and notice that I only used one name for each. You want people to have a perception of you based on your performance, knowledge, and accomplishments. This applies in corporate America and for entrepreneurial business owners. Creating and refining your personal brand is vital to monetizing your passion online and offline. Personal branding is relevant in your professional life and your personal life.

The approach of "under promise and over deliver" gives people confidence in you. Be consistently polished in your communications and appearance as you build your personal brand.

Here is an example of the implications of personal branding. Let us assume you work in the Sales Department of your firm. In a Sales environment, your revenue goal is your main objective. However, you are also on a Sales Team. If you overdeliver, you exceed your goal. And you are perceived as a great team player because someone else might fall short of their goal. The team still wins. Thus, the benefit is two-fold. In this type of scenario, your personal brand becomes the following: *we can count on you.*

Have you ever purchased a ticket in the rafters, only to end up sitting in the lower bowl? How did you feel when you received such excellent service? That feeling should be exactly what you try to deliver to others in your professional career and your personal life.

However, sometimes the brand falls flat. And it can happen very quickly.

Adidas has a strong global brand built on a passion for sports and a sporting lifestyle. They have excellent products and enjoy a great image. But how would you feel about the brand if – after training for six months – you were running a marathon and your Adidas shoes fell apart at Mile 13? If this hypothetical example came to pass, what would you do for the 2nd half of the race to finish the 26.2 miles?

Here is a way to think of it. Your LinkedIn page is *generally* "equivalent" to the millions of dollars that Adidas spends on advertising. It is the same purpose. You are telling the audience what they can expect about you.

Look to mentors, real and virtual, that you can follow as examples. And when you perform well, other people will tell your story.

Make sure your digital footprint is refined, or at least intentionally reflects what you want your brand promise to be. On LinkedIn, have a professional headshot in high resolution. In addition, do a background photo, maybe with your company logo, if you are a business owner. Your headline message on LinkedIn must be compelling. Use short videos that reflect your brand promise to give your LinkedIn profile some sizzle. Get action-orientated recommendations from reputable people.

As you build your personal brand, be careful not to disparage anyone on any social media sites. Debating ideas is one thing; personal attacks are something else. Think of your social media posts, pictures, videos, and comments as a reflection of your brand. Since social media is meant to be social, in the past, I typically made sure that, at least, 80% of what I post is lifestyle content that has nothing to do with the business interests I am pursuing. However, these days, the desired mix does depend on the specific social media platform. If you want to heavily focus on business, you may want to consider having a separate Facebook page for your business or a second Instagram account. These days, social media and life are heavily intertwined. Systems are changing. For Millennials (a.k.a. Gen Y, born 1981 to 1996) and for the younger Gen Z (born 1995 to 2015), social media is even more important and impactful than it is for older folks.

You also need a blog so that your message cuts through the chatter. Set it up so that each blog post automatically goes to your social media pages, as appropriate. Go to WordPress or Tumblr to get started. This is a great way to find your voice. A few paragraphs from my past blog posts actually served as inspirations for specific chapters in this book that you are enjoying now.

And think about what you stand for – not just your function, such as marketing or engineering. Let people know about what you value, such as community service, leadership, or mentoring. What are you passionate about? Do the work to back up what you say.

Everyone must begin to think of themselves as a brand. A lot of people talk about what they intend to do. However, that is irrelevant if no action is taken. Just do it now!

"Quickest way to build trust: Keep promises you make, don't over-promise. Over-deliver, don't under-deliver. If you say you'll do something, make sure you do but if things then run late or go wrong, tell your client at the earliest opportunity."

— Phil Harding, author, and photographer

#DoItNow – What Actions Will You Take as a Result of Reading This Chapter?
1)
2)
3)

CHAPTER TWENTY-FIVE

ALL WE DO IS WIN,
NO MATTER WHAT

---

*"My attitude is never to be satisfied,
never enough, never."*

— Duke Ellington, composer, pianist,
and jazz orchestra leader

Vince Lombardi, the victorious coach of the Green Bay Packers in the first two Super Bowls, said, "Winning is not a sometime thing; it's an all the time thing. You don't win once in a while; you don't do things right once in a while; you do them right all of the time. Winning is a habit. Unfortunately, so is losing."

When you win, there is nothing more that you have to say. No need for excuses or apologies. Leave those things to others, including those that failed to reach their goal and those who missed the deadline.

> **Life Lesson:**
> When you win, there is nothing more that you have to say. No need for excuses or apologies.

In the rare instances that you do lose:

- Learn from your occasional losses
- If you fail to reach a goal, that does not define you as a failure; just believe you will win next time
- Always come back after practicing with enhanced tenacity, skills, and performance

Lombardi also taught, *"Leaders aren't born, they are made. They are made by hard effort, which is the price all of us must pay to achieve any goal that is worthwhile."* Lombardi knew how to win, which is why the Super Bowl trophy is now named after him.

Besides the things Lombardi mentioned – habits (see Chapter Five for more) and hard work (see Chapter Six for more) – how can we lead efficiently and win more often? Here is a framework. Think of your status at any given time as one of the following:

- Reaction
- Contemplation
- Creativity

A definition of reactive is acting in response to a situation rather than generating or controlling it – letting circumstances and conditions control your response to the matter. When you are in this state, you lack the proactive creativity you need to advance your dreams. Reactive people are like the supporting cast actors in a feature film, just feebly following a script they did not write.

A meaning of contemplation is to look at something thoughtfully for a long time. At first glance, that does not sound so bad if the intent is to process previous occurrences so you can improve future performance.

However, this state focuses on past events, and we know the past cannot be changed. One can become preoccupied with perceived mistakes, losses, or actions taken or not taken. There is a risk of developing feelings of regret, anger, or envy. Some people become frozen and take no decisive action.

Creativity is using the imagination or original ideas to get something done. When your status is in the creativity zone, you are proactive in the pursuit of your definite major purpose (DMP) and other important goals. Hockey great, Wayne Gretzky, explains, "I skate to where the puck is going to be, not where it has been." Baseball coaches help fielders handle hard ground balls by saying, "play the ball before it plays you." This means you want to be proactive and make a good play by moving forward and catching the ball at its apex, not letting the ball get on top of you and handcuff you.

I view Elon Musk, co-founder and CEO of Tesla, as a proactive example of a category creator. In the electric vehicle marketplace specifically, Tesla has essentially *created a luxury and style category*. Musk figuratively skated to where he perceived the puck was going to be.

Long before Tesla, legend has it that when proactive creator, Henry Ford, asked potential customers what they wanted, they said they just wanted faster horses. Ford eventually created the Model T in 1908 and went on to develop the assembly line mode of production, which transformed the auto industry. Ford created the first automobile that middle-class Americans could afford, which was a truly new category at the time.

The stock market is home for people in each status category mentioned previously in this chapter. Think about the days or weeks when there were massive losses for stocks on Wall Street. The reactive people sell off their stocks or mutual funds *after* they tank. Generally, they take a loss.

Those in a state of obsessive contemplation generally take no action at all. They just worry a lot. They are often stuck.

However, the proactive people can find bargains during such scary times – companies with strong fundamentals whose stock prices are poised to shoot up on the next wave of positive economic news that *will* inevitably come. Think about what billionaire investor, Warren Buffet, usually does during a downturn in stock prices. He is in it for the long haul.

When you are in a state of creativity with your life or your business endeavors, you do not look to fight for a piece of a limited, scarce pie. You *expand the pie* before you divide it. Or, even better, you create new pies.

Life Lesson:

When you are in a state of creativity you do not look to fight for a piece of a limited, scarce pie. You expand the pie before you divide it – or you create new pies.

To get more than your fair share of the available pie, you must get your mindset right. Winning and success come from belief. The correct order is BE, then DO, then HAVE. Almost 2000 years ago,

Greek philosopher, Epictetus, said, "First say to yourself what you would be; and then do what you have to do."

There is a distinction between so-called important things and things that *really make the difference*. We all do a lot of "good and important" things, for example, taking your child to weekly math tutoring. That is good if your child needs tutoring. However, often, we do not do what really makes a difference because it involves a big risk or a huge challenge. For example, starting a new entrepreneurial endeavor could involve some risk. Likewise, going to graduate school might be an enormous challenge in many ways. When you want to do something that really makes the difference, you often want to take on a new way of *being*. Then you can *do* more and, ultimately, *have* more.

Life Lesson:

There is a distinction between so-called important things and things that really make the difference.

Creatively challenge your ideas about what you can and cannot do. To reach your dream, what attributes do you need to personify? If someone wants to become a doctor, they might take on a way of *being* as committed to helping others or maybe *being* dedicated. If someone wants to be a teacher that helps more students achieve greatness, they might want to take on a character of *being* inspirational.

The so-called important things must be done, but it is just an excuse if we let those important things stop us from doing the profound thing or things that *really make the difference*. Remember, if your status is in the creativity zone, you are proactive in your pursuit of your definite major purpose (DMP) and other important goals. This means you are more likely to do the things that can really make the difference. Yes, you still need to do the so-called important task of washing and folding the laundry each week, for example. However, the laundry should not stop you from achieving your DMP.

Take a moment for yourself to think about the handful of things that *really made a profound difference in your own life* so far. Even though I have lived a lot of years, for me, it has only been about 7 or 8 things that come to mind:

- As an infant, I was adopted by a great family in Pittsburgh, and then in my twenties, I found my biological families, descending from both Europe and Africa.
- I worked hard to be my high school's valedictorian, which enabled me to get scholarships and attend the very well-regarded University of Pittsburgh School of Engineering. I graduated from college debt-free.
- During college, I secured four summer internships in corporate America related to my major, thanks to a great organization called INROADS. This accelerated my career.
- I pledged Alpha Phi Alpha Fraternity, Inc. – giving me more great friendships and a huge national network of successful Brothers.
- I earned my Master of Business Administration (MBA) degree by age 25 from the highly ranked University of Maryland Smith Business School.
- I learned to negotiate, which enabled me to get more money while I was in corporate America and still greatly helps me now that I am a business owner.

- I married my wonderful wife, Nikki, and we raised our children, which means everything to me.

Do what *really makes the difference*, despite the risk or the challenge. If you really want to grow and win, you must put yourself in a quandary – real or imagined. A quandary will push you to grow by taking on a new way of being. And you cannot win if there is no battle.

For example, someone who owns a part-time business may be going through the motions as an entrepreneur as long as they have a steady paycheck from their corporate day job. However, if they were to be laid off, that quandary would lead to a sense of urgency about their part-time business. In this situation, this person should take proactive, creative action for their part-time business *while* they still have a day job. It is all about a different state of being. In this case, the person needs to be urgent and proactive. You always have a choice about your way of being. Dig the well before you need the water. Challenge the status quo of a "mediocre life of contemplation."

Proactively create and be in action. Sure, the action you take might be wrong. You can then, of course, correct. It is similar to riding a bicycle when you lean back and forth but rarely fall completely.

A related guiding principle espoused by former UCLA coach, John Wooden – winner of 10 NCAA basketball national championships – is Competitive Greatness. This phrase means you have a real love for the hard battle knowing that it offers you the opportunity to be at your best when your best is required. You want to deliver your peak performance when greatness is essential. You must be results-oriented. If you love what you do, you should enjoy a challenge.

If you care about winning, your life will not be happy if you are not producing.

Life Lesson:

If you care about winning, your life will not be happy if you are not producing.

An important part of winning is leaving a legacy. Leaving a legacy is defined in various ways, depending on the person. Some people think it involves achieving something that makes you famous or maybe obtaining and leaving behind great material wealth. There is nothing wrong with those types of things. I even see my own books that I have written as being part of my legacy – my stories will live on even after I am gone.

However, when I think about legacy, I specifically focus on the impact I can have on other people during my years on this planet. Someone can create a large estate and pass it down to their loved ones while still not leaving an impactful legacy. If you do not connect with and positively influence your family before you pass, your family just remembers the money you left behind. You want them to remember you for the memories created along the way. Leaving a legacy behind can involve leaving some resources for future generations, but you hope that money is not the first thing someone thinks of when they remember you.

The legacy I want to leave behind starts with the people close to me. My goal is to influence and assist others so they can achieve a greater level of success than I did. And it does not matter what that level of success ends up being. If your only legacy is money, it is possible that your "legacy" will eventually run out one day.

Alternately, if you taught and influenced others on how to be independently successful, they can make their own money and, hopefully, leave their own legacies in terms of both wealth and the people they mentored. The legacy that I am chasing includes memories and lessons for those around me. I care more about things that matter, like personal development, happiness, and security. Congruent with my vision for my world, I want to leave others with the opportunity to achieve a life of fun, fulfilling relationships, autonomy, community service, legacy, and financial security.

The best way to achieve extraordinary performance and happiness for yourself is to want and work toward extraordinary performance and happiness for everyone.

Life Lesson:

To achieve extraordinary performance and happiness for yourself, work toward extraordinary performance and happiness for everyone.

As long as I had a real influence on my children and left a true impact on others so that they are in a better position, going forward, I know that I will leave a true legacy for the future and that my life mattered.

You can win and leave a prominent legacy. Just do it now!

"Define success on your own terms, achieve it by your own rules, and build a life you're proud to live."

— Anne Sweeney, former President of the Disney–ABC Television Group

#DoItNow – What Actions Will You Take as a Result of Reading This Chapter?
1)
2)
3)

CHAPTER TWENTY-SIX

DO IT NOW

"Progress rarely comes as a result of being passive."

— Marc Morial, President of the National Urban
League and former Mayor of New Orleans

Time marches on. Quickly get clarity on your goals and dreams. You do not want to lead a life where you are not clear about what you are committed to. If you choose to delay the proactive pursuit of your dreams, you will never get that time back. Just do it now!

We cannot trust our "feelings". We must be disciplined when it comes to taking action on the tasks to accomplish our goals. Even if you do not feel like taking action, just do it now. If you only take proactive action on days that you feel good, you will not be very productive. It is not about how you feel; instead, it is about what you are committed to accomplishing.

Moreover, if you have the discipline to make your actions control your feelings and thoughts, you will get a lot more done, and you will "feel" better in the end. For example, I may have an hour in my schedule to reach out to potential clients, which I normally am happy to do. However, on some days, I may not "feel" like making those phone calls. I learned that if I just take action and talk to the predetermined number of people, I always "feel" great after I am done.

Life Lesson:

If you only take proactive action on days that you feel good, you will not be very productive. It is not about how you feel; it is about what you are committed to accomplishing.

Put everything in your schedule that is necessary to reach your dreams, then honor your schedule. Everyone gets the same 168 hours each week. Powerful folks are just people that are afraid, but they act, nevertheless.

Life Lesson:

Powerful folks are just people that are afraid, but they act, nevertheless.

Napoleon Hill wrote, "Don't wait. The time will never be just right." And Robert Anthony adds, "Waiting is a trap. There will always be reasons to wait – The truth is, there are only two things in life, reasons and results, and reasons simply don't count."

If you want different results, make the choice to take on a new way of being. You can do this anytime you want. Do you want to have more passion, a stronger sense of urgency, or more integrity? Or maybe you want to create a persona of fearlessness?

After all, the place is here. The time is now. Live and act in the present moment. Today is all we have. We must put the past in the past. I guarantee you cannot change the past. All we have is right now, and the actions and decisions of now impact our future. Your future can be almost anything you want it to be.

Life Lesson:

Live and act in the present moment. Today is all we have. We must put the past in the past. I guarantee you cannot change the past.

After you develop some (not necessarily all) skills in your area of expertise, just take the shot.

Here is a way to think of it. If I place 100 basketballs on racks at the half-court line and tell you to take 100 shots from there, most people will make less than five. Some people will not make any shots.

However, if I move you up to the three-point line and tell you to take 100 shots, your shooting percentage will surely improve. Finally, I put you on the free-throw line; you will probably make at least half of your shots. And if you practice 100 free throws every day for months, your shooting percentage will increase. It is the same distance from the basket, but you make more shots. You are getting better through practice.

Every time you seek and gain a new skill, you move closer to the basket. So, keep adding skills, but do not wait until some mythical time when you will "know everything" before you take action. Just take the shot.

Some people never take any shots. And some people take a few shots, miss their target, get discouraged, and quit on their own dreams. Are they afraid to hear the word "no"? What if you were not afraid of "no"? If you fail, just fail fast. Try again or create something new.

From President Theodore Roosevelt, "In a moment of decision, the best thing you can do is the right thing to do, the next best thing is the wrong thing, and the worst thing you can do is nothing."

Just take the shot. "You miss 100% of the shots you don't take," observed Wayne Gretzky, hockey Hall of Famer. And I would add that you must follow up the shot. Just as following up the shot helps you collect the rebound and score in hockey or basketball, follow up in your life and career to enable your great achievement.

Your very best is good enough. Try your absolute best in all situations that matter to you. Do not worry about what you cannot control. Worrying does not help. Action is what helps.

Life Lesson:

Your very best is good enough. Try your absolute best in all situations that matter to you.

If you fail on a specific task, that does not make you a failure overall. If you miss a shot, readjust and fire again. The two questions to ask when you fail to reach a particular goal are: What can I learn from this failure that will help me in the future? What actions do I need to complete next?

After you know your next steps, replace any procrastination with action.

Author Og Mandino summed it up well, "My procrastination, which has held me back, was born of fear, and now I recognize this secret mined from the depths of courageous hearts. Now, I know that to conquer fear, I must always act without hesitation, and the flutters in my heart will vanish. Now, I know that action reduces the lion of terror to an ant of equanimity."

In 2005, we planted an orange tree in our backyard. It is now nearly 30 feet high, and it consistently produces a huge crop of fruit during the months from November to January. Recently, I decided to plant two apple trees, two pear trees, and two plum trees. We have a big yard. I wish I had planted the apples, pears, and plums 15 years ago, but the second-best time is *right now*. So, I took action to get started on other types of fruit.

Life Lesson:

Two years from now or maybe five years from now, depending on your specific dream, you will wish you started today.

What is your big dream? What is your definite major purpose? Two years from now or maybe five years from now, depending on your specific dream, you will wish you started *today*. Just do it now!

> "If there's a book you really want to read but it hasn't been written yet, then you must write it."

> — Toni Morrison, Nobel, and Pulitzer Prize -winning novelist

#DoItNow – What Actions Will You Take as a Result of Reading This Chapter?
1)
2)
3)

CHAPTER (26.2)

PRIORITIZE FUN AS YOU FINISH THE RACE

"Just play; have fun; enjoy the game."

— Michael Jordan, 6-time NBA Champion

Near the end of a marathon, after you get to Mile 26, you still have 0.2 miles to go. Specifically, your remaining distance is 385 yards. Never forget the final 385 yards. It is short but memorable and fun, especially since you can see the finish line.

In this short final chapter, I want to remind you to *prioritize fun*. Live your best life. Live to the fullest and savor it while you can. Work hard and play hard. You deserve it. Life is too short to not have a ton of fun.

Life Lesson:

Prioritize fun. Live your best life. Live to the fullest and savor it while you can. Work hard and play hard. You deserve it. Life is too short to not have a ton of fun.

If you can make your career or entrepreneurial endeavors congruent with what you view as fun, you will be a much happier person over the long haul. *"People rarely succeed unless they have fun in what they are doing,"* according to Dale Carnegie. If you are not having fun, you should investigate whether there is another career or business that may provide both the fun and the success you need and deserve. Achievement is only half of the journey; having fun is the remaining half.

> **Life Lesson:**
>
> To prioritize fun, make fun a part of your vision, a part of your very definition of success.

Put yourself in workplace or entrepreneurial situations where you enjoy being around your colleagues. If you can have fun with the team as you complete your daily tasks, the work goes faster, and you typically achieve more. People – and managers – tend to be impressed by someone who is earning money and having fun.

You can also integrate your fun with your community service. One charitable cause I care about is fighting Multiple Sclerosis (MS). MS is a progressive neurological disorder that affects people in many different ways. It could be paralysis one day, loss of vision the next, or impaired memory the day after that. Living with MS means living with uncertainty. I am particularly inspired to raise money to fight MS because I have a cousin and some very good friends who have been diagnosed with MS. I have committed, for over 10 straight years, to participating in the MS150 – riding a bike with over 10,000 other cyclists more than 150 miles in a weekend to help raise money to make a difference. I typically raise over $2500 each year as I train for and complete the challenging ride. I have an amazing time during the two-day event. Tents are set up for our overnight stay outside a small Texas town. It is a huge fun party at the end of both days. I want to continue to participate in the MS150 for as long as I am able.

And finally, assess your 'fun factor' on a regular basis. Of course, every day cannot be a party because there are tasks to get done and clients to satisfy. However, I do challenge myself to do something special and fun every month or two, even if it is a simple thing like a visit to a local beach or a new restaurant. And to inspire you, just know that I have been to nearly 40 countries and all seven continents. I have visited all 50 U.S. states. I attended toga parties as an undergraduate student and hosted 'Pajama Jam' themed house parties as an adult. I performed in fraternity step shows, and I was crowned Homecoming King in the bicentennial year for my university. I skied in Austria, Canada, and across the USA. I parasailed in France, dove from a cliff in Jamaica, and skydived in Indiana. From white water rafting to NASCAR, from Independence Hall in Philadelphia to The Forbidden City in Beijing, from Niagara Falls in North America to Iguazu Falls in South America. I love to have fun.

Maybe you are wondering – is that it for your 'fun factor'? Well, if you need more inspiration, be mindful that I have attended the Super Bowl, the NBA Finals, the World Series, the Stanley Cup Finals, the U.S. Open golf tournament, the Final Four, the World Cup quarterfinals, and four Olympiads. I scuba dove at the Great Barrier Reef and attended multiple photo safaris in Kenya/Tanzania. From Bourbon Street in New Orleans for Mardi Gras to the amazing Carnival in Rio de Janeiro, I have been known to enjoy a good party.

I have been to the Great Wall of China and the Grand Canyon. I am fortunate to have some of the best and most supportive friends in the world. I proposed to my wife at the top of the tram at Heavenly Ski Resort, overlooking Lake Tahoe. And most importantly, I have been there for my kids to support their academic, social, and emotional growth – I coached my son's teams in youth basketball and football. I enjoyed watching my daughter's participation in soccer and on cheer and tumbling teams. And that is just the tip of the iceberg.

What is fun for you? Maybe it is playing Spades. Perhaps it is a girls' or a guys' night out. Seriously, what is fun for you: sitting on the beach, reading a book? Watching a Grand Slam tennis match? Cooking an Indian meal from a new cookbook? Joining your girlfriends for a spa day? Tailgating at a college football game? Walking and shopping on the Miracle Mile in Chicago? Joining a neighborhood book club? Spending a week in NYC watching a different show each night on Broadway? Running a marathon on the beach in California? Watching the ball drop on New Year's Eve in Times Square? Clubbing in London? Riding a gondola in Venice? Going on a tour of famous church buildings throughout Europe? Taking in art by the masters at a famous museum? Visiting the Vatican? Seeing the pyramids in Egypt? Driving across the US in a convertible from coast-to-coast? Watching a Formula One race in Europe? Visiting the Sydney Opera House? Hanging out at home with your family? Find what makes you ecstatically happy and do it.

Let's go crazy! Prioritize fun!

Life is a marathon, not a sprint – don't get it twisted. It is my hope that this book gives you the mindset and motivation to be a powerful, unstoppable force as you achieve your dreams. Apply these 26.2 life lessons in your world to access the treasures of sustainable happiness and success that await you at the finish line.

Just do it now!

"Funny how time flies when you're having fun. I don't know where it all went. Time passed us by. Just when it seemed the fun began."

— Janet Jackson, 5-time Grammy Award-winning singer and actress

#DoItNow – What Actions Will You Take as a Result of Reading This Chapter?
1)
2)
3)

ALPHA MULTIMEDIA, INC.
COMPANY PROFILE

Would it be OK if we help you create a polished brand without investing a lot of time?

Boost your brand recognition, resulting in more leads, customers, and revenue.

Imagine for a moment if you could:

- Get more buzz and media coverage without a huge expense

- Get valuable help with marketing and public relations for your product, service, or book

- Generate other streams of income beyond what you're already doing

- Get more people to already know about your products and services before you call them

- Find a dynamic trainer, workshop facilitator, or motivational keynote speaker

We'll show you how to do all that... and more!

What We Do:

We deliver results by manically focusing on our clients – small & midsize businesses (SMB), non-profits, schools, universities, authors & publishers. We help you enhance your brand so that you can grow your revenues faster.

Next Step – Book a Free Consultation:

Book a free 1-hour Zoom consultation so that we can get you on the path to creating more awareness within your target audience and additional sales leads to grow your business. Go to **AlphaMultimedia.com** or call +1 (281) 217-1960 now.

ABOUT THE AUTHOR

Thomas Brooks is the Founder of Alpha Multimedia, Inc., a marketing, public relations, and public speaking firm. He brings over 20 years of marketing and PR experience to this business. He previously worked in marketing roles for Hewlett-Packard (HP), Lucent Technologies, and Texas Instruments. Brooks has been published more than twenty times, and he has participated in panel discussions at many trade shows. He has been featured in articles, on the radio, and on TV. He won the annual *Career Communications Magazine* national award for "Excellence in Technical Sales and Marketing."

Brooks earned his B.S. Electrical Engineering from the University of Pittsburgh and his MBA from the University of Maryland. His first book, *A Wealth of Family: An Adopted Son's International Quest for Heritage, Reunion, and Enrichment*, was an Amazon bestseller in its category and was named a "Best Books" Award Winner by USA Book News. His second book, *26.2 Ways to Do It Now: Life Lessons for Happiness and Success*, launched in 2021.

As a John Maxwell Certified Coach, Teacher, Trainer and Speaker, Brooks can offer you workshops, seminars, keynote speaking, and coaching, aiding your personal and professional growth through study and practical application of John Maxwell's proven leadership methods.

Brooks is a life member of Alpha Phi Alpha Fraternity, Inc., and the National Black MBA Association. He enjoys public speaking, snow skiing, and cycling. He lives with his wife and children near Houston, Texas, USA.

www.ingramcontent.com/pod-product-compliance
Lightning Source LLC
LaVergne TN
LVHW051254080426
835509LV00020B/2971